UNANSWERED QUESTIONS

UNANSWERED QUESTIONS

Theological Views of Jewish-Catholic Relations

EDITED BY ROGER BROOKS

University of Notre Dame Press
Notre Dame, Indiana

Library of Congress Cataloging-in-Publication Data

Unanswered questions.

1. Catholic Church—Relations—Judaism.   2.
Judaism—Relations—Catholic Church.   3. Vati-
can Council (2nd : 1962-1965). Declaratio de
ecclesiae habitudine ad religiones non-
Christianas.
I. Brooks, Roger.
BM535.U53   1988   261.2'6   87-40353
ISBN 0-268-01902-9

FOR JACOB NEUSNER

Contents

III. TWENTY YEARS OF PROGRESS

IV. THE FUTURE AGENDA

Acknowledgments

I extend my thanks to many colleagues who played a role in this project as authors, advisors, or participants. I express particular gratitude to those in the Department of Theology at the University of Notre Dame who make my job so enjoyable: Chairman Richard McBrien, who encourages and fosters my work in Judaica, and Assistant Chairwoman F. Ellen Weaver, for her aid in planning and executing programs in Jewish and Christian relations. By their example, they show the mutual respect necessary for the development of beneficial interaction between Judaism and Christianity. It goes without saying that I appreciate as well the true interest shown by all my other colleagues in the department.

Rabbi Leon Klenicki of the Anti-Defamation League of B'nai B'rith kindly served as critical reader. His perspective as director of the Division of Interfaith Affairs contributed many insights and added to the theological dimension of this volume.

I dedicate this volume to Professor Jacob Neusner, my teacher and friend. His entire career has been devoted to asserting the centrality and importance of Judaic Studies in the broad setting of the University. By bringing Judaica before the general public, he has contributed immeasurably to scholarly exchange and healthy relations between Christians and Jews.

As my teacher and mentor, I gratefully acknowledge his tutelege: without the training I received from him and the vision that guides our entire field, neither this book nor the conference on which it is based would have seen the light of day.

Roger Brooks
Tu B'Shevat 5747

A tree planted toward
continued close relations
between Judaism and
Christianity

Introduction: Unanswered Questions and Unquestioned Answers

ROGER BROOKS

When Alice stepped through the looking glass into Wonderland, she found reflected in that mirror an odd empire indeed. Unfamiliar faces and creatures confronted her, instead of the comforting sameness she knew from the small world in which she grew up. Until 1965, much the same situation faced Jews and Catholics who attempted to look out through their own windows and to glimpse a bit of the others' world. Jews sometimes saw Catholics as among those who stood by during the mass murders in Nazi Germany; Catholics saw Jews, it seemed, as those who had killed God's own begotten Son. Jews saw Catholics as endlessly desiring their conversion and disappearance as a people; Catholics saw Jews as easy targets of hatred and as scapegoats.

In many ways, all that changed twenty years ago, when the Second Vatican Council issued its proclamation entitled *Nostra Aetate*. This pronouncement in dramatic language stated that,

> The Jews still remain most dear to God because of their fathers, for He does not repent of the gifts He makes nor of the calls He issues (cf. Rom. 11:28–29). . . . Since the spir-

1

itual patrimony common to Christians and Jews is thus so great, this sacred Synod wishes to foster and recommend that mutual understanding and respect which is the fruit above all of biblical and theological studies, and of brotherly dialogues.

Today, twenty years later, these words have changed the way that Jews and Catholics live together. On every level of social interaction, from neighborhood to church and synagogue to Vatican and State, real progress has been made in the manner in which we treat one another. In this spirit, the papers brought together in this book celebrate two decades of dialogue.

This book had its beginnings in a conference held at the University of Notre Dame, October 28–29, 1985. It is fitting to quote here from the original statement of that conference:

> *"Nostra Aetate. . . . "* these words open the Declaration on the Relationship of the Church to Non-Christian Religions issued by the Second Vatican Council on October 28, 1965. Although the document made reference to other non-Christian religions, it responded directly to the request of Pope John XXIII in 1963 that the Council issue a state-ment on the Jews. When his successor, Pope Paul VI, signed and promulgated the document, a major improvement occurred in the often tragic history of Jews and Christians. The document provided a positive theology of the ongoing role of the Jewish people in salvation history, and, at the same time, repudiated anti-Semitism.

> Twenty years later, this symposium brings together scholars and religious leaders. The goal of the symposium is three-fold: (1) to survey the history of the document, including how the various theological questions were posed, how they were solved, and what compromises were made; (2) to con-sider official developments since the Council, and how the document affected theological inquiry and especially

Catholic and Jewish religious education; (3) to ask what theological issues remain, and what we can project for the future.

Most of these papers have been rewritten to take into account comments and discussions at the conference, and I have arranged them so as to produce a useful guide to the beginner in the dialogue between Jews and Christians. At the same time, I have tried to allow the three main interests of the conference—history, progress, and future agenda—to remain at the forefront. Above all, though, these papers stand out for their theological perspective on *Nostra Aetate*. In this book the reader will find unique reflections upon the entire range of theological issues of importance in contemporary Judaism and Christianity, all refracted through the Jewish-Christian dialogue. This larger interest constitutes the distinctive viewpoint and contribution of this volume.

THE HISTORY OF *NOSTRA AETATE*

A wide range of events shaped the Declaration *Nostra Aetate*: political maneuvers and blunders, personal pleas and commitments. So too the theological impulses that led the Church to its desire to issue this statement varied from the Church's acknowledgment of the errors inherent in the traditional teaching of contempt for Jews to new understandings of Paul's Epistle to the Romans.

The three papers in section two spell out these many factors. In "Holy Diplomacy: Making the Impossible Possible," Father Thomas F. Stransky traces five years of tortuous ups and downs within the Secretariat for Promoting Christian Unity, the body that drafted *Nostra Aetate*. He claims that the declaration emerged perhaps too early from the viewpoint of Catholic theology, yet too late to save millions of Jewish lives from Nazi death camps. He documents these claims with the authority commanded only by a direct participant in the drafting. He explains step-by-step what had gone on behind the scenes in the Vatican and so leads the reader to a full appreciation of the leap forward marked by this "bold and clear, yet in hindsight also timid and unaware" document.

If Stransky lays out the historical influences on the formation of *Nostra Aetate*, then Wendell S. Dietrich's *"Nostra Aetate:* A Typology of Theological Tendencies" clearly shows the same materials viewed from a fresh, analytic position. Dietrich "leap[s] over the narrative chronicle of the stages of *Nostra Aetate's* formulation and look[s] directly at the completed text." In that text, he discerns four separate theological impulses that propelled the Church in its desire to create *Nostra Aetate*:

> First, simple affirmative declaration about the Jews in acknowledgment of the errors of the traditional teaching of contempt for the Jews; second, a social ethical impulse grounded in the necessity for mutual respect among various social groups that are in increasingly close interaction in modern global society; third, a new positive attitude toward non-Christian religions accompanied by a general theory of non-Christian religions; and, fourth and finally, a Christian theology of Judaism based on a fresh reading of the Pauline teaching about the Jews in Romans 9–11.

Dietrich's paper is refreshing in its clarity and precision. It also challenges both Christians and Jews to respond to a sharp and critical observation that Christians and Christianity in general seem to be preoccupied with Jews. Perhaps the most interesting moment in the paper is when Dietrich muses that the Jews ought to revel in their liberation from such Christian preoccupation.

Stranky's and Dietrich's papers stand together for another reason: both speak at length about the proper interpretation of Romans 9–11. These chapters spell out one stage in the slow but sure process of separation between Jews and Christians. To this day, their image of a branch grafted onto a tree remains generative of current theology, up to and including the most recent statements of the Vatican's Commission for Religious Relations with the Jews. This sort of examination of the outsider, entirely parallel to rabbinic examinations carried out at the same time in Mishnah tractate *Avodah Zarah,* reveals crucial information about the theological understanding of the early church.

Rabbi Daniel Polish completes this trio of papers examining the historical, theological, and political influences on *Nostra Aetate* by looking at Jewish contributions to the document's formulation. He points to the central role of importance played by Rabbi Abraham Joshua Heschel. Polish traces several years of meetings between Heschel and Vatican leaders and briefly comments upon the impact of this man.

In addition, Polish portrays the varied reactions within the Jewish community to the very notion of dialogue with Catholics. On the one side, he presents the possibly overly sympathetic view of Maurice Eisendrath:

> We Jews have long clamored for this indispensable change in official Catholic dissemination of fact and interpretation. . . . But what about our Jewish attitudes toward Christendom, toward Jesus especially? . . . How long before we can admit that His influence was a beneficial one, not only to the pagans, but to the Jews of his time as well, and that only those who later took His name in vain profaned his teaching?

As Polish notes, it would be hard to imagine a more generous and warm invitation to enter into dialogue, and to base that dialogue on the desire to right mutual past wrongs.

The other side of Jewish opinion in the early 1960s Polish finds represented in a statement by Norman Lamm:

As Jews we object to being absolved of the guilt of killing their God. To be absolved implies that one is guilty, but that he nevertheless is being forgiven. . . . To our mind the question is not who will absolve the Jews. The question is, who will absolve the Church for its guilt in inspiring and sponsoring crusades and inquisitions, blood libels and pogroms. The Church has expressed to the Jewish people neither apology nor confessions nor regrets.

The point-counterpoint represented by these two statements speaks for itself.

TWENTY YEARS OF PROGRESS

The papers in section three of the book have a different goal and tenor. Here we find papers aimed at assessing the theological progress made in the dialogue during the twenty years that have passed since the publication of *Nostra Aetate*.

Michael Signer's paper, "*Speculum Concilii*: Through the Mirror Brightly," traces two twisted strands: (1) what Jews and Catholics have accomplished, and (2) what remains ahead in the dialogue. Throughout his contribution, the controlling metaphor is that Jews and Catholics each may serve as a mirror for the other. We see ourselves best when we see each other. Hence, Signer notes, Jews and Catholics have served as goads to each other's conscience, as partners in an upper-level exchange that has seen real improvements in the realms of priests' and rabbis' study-groups, textbooks, and the outlines of a new relationship.

Signer also notes some backsliding, and this surely will displease some who would like to present the last twenty years only in a positive light. "When I attended religious school, more than twenty five years ago," says Signer, "we attended Christian worship with both Catholics and Protestants. . . . My children attend that same synagogue

school . . . [but] have not experienced any worship outside the Jewish environment." In sum, Signer urges that
what has taken place at the highest levels of the dialogue—namely real improvement in relations—has yet
to filter down to the grass roots. "During the next twenty
years, our mission is to communicate the outlines of our
new relationship to the broadest possible audience," including those intimately involved in religious education
at every level.

Urging this same dissemination of information to
"seminaries, classrooms, pulpits, and streets," Father Edward Flannery's paper echoes virtually all of Signer's
comments. In fact, these two form a matched set. For
Flannery, anti-Semitism constitutes both the gain in the
past twenty years and the agenda for the next. "Christian
anti-Semitism took root in Christian theology and to
some degree is still nourished by it today." Thanks to
strides made in the past, "virtually all agree that any
Christian theological consideration of Judaism must include a full appreciation of the Jewish heritage of Christianity, of the Jewishness of Jesus and the primitive
church, of the rejection of offensive teachings."

Taking anti-Semitism as the first issue on the agenda,
Flannery proceeds through virtually all of the tough
issues, noting where progress has been made and where
substantial work remains. Theology, the Holocaust, and
the State of Israel—on these issues within the debate,
Flannery claims we have done acceptably; yet precisely
these same issues are the ones he wishes to see remain on
the agenda. And, like Signer, Flannery sees the extension
of that agenda to the masses as crucial.

THE FUTURE AGENDA

John T. Pawlikowski's short paper, "A Theology of
Religious Pluralism?" takes its cue from Signer's image of
a mirror. He moves into the question of the future agen-

da for Jewish and Catholic relations, urging that the two traditions develop a constructive theology of religious pluralism. Critical to this development, according to Pawlikowski, is the awareness that neither tradition has an exclusive hold on truth. He urges that Jews and Christians begin to reevaluate their eschatological truth claims, admitting the possibility of the others' co-existence. On the Christian side, this involves the recognition of four principles:

> (1) The Christ event did not invalidate the Jewish faith perspective; (2) Christianity is not superior to Judaism, nor is it the fulfillment of Judaism, as previously maintained; (3) the Sinai covenant is in principle as crucial to Christian faith expression as the covenant in Christ; and (4) Christianity needs to reincorporate dimensions from its original Jewish context.

Pawlikowski's focus on the issue of religious pluralism takes us a step further, by showing just how interconnected were many of the theological discussions of the Second Vatican Council. For religious pluralism was not only a vital issue with regard to Jewish-Christian relations, but also in the sphere of religious freedom in general. Pawlikowski thus attends to issues raised in *Nostra Aetate,* but also reflects the concerns of the *Declaration on Religious Liberty.*

The last three papers move beyond Pawlikowski and boldly take up issues critical to the future of Jewish and Catholic dialogue. Each takes as its starting point the recent "Notes on the Correct Way to Present the Jews and Judaism in Preaching and Catechesis in the Roman Catholic Church" (May, 1985). Yet the papers differ strikingly.

David Burrell takes up Karl Rahner's challenge that Vatican II marked as dramatic a change in Judaism and Christianity as did the destruction of the Temple in 70 C.E. According to Burrell, Christians must grasp that "the issues which emerged in the 'parting of the ways' remain formative for Christians' understanding of themselves." Jews, by the same token, must learn to get over their complete preoccupation with Israel, because "the Middle East conflict tends so totally to absorb contemporary Jewish discussion as to place larger issues of self-understanding at risk, to say nothing of Jewish self-understanding in relation to Christianity." Burrell then procedes to interpret the 1985 "Notes'" references to the State of Israel in a highly positive, and most suggestive, light.

In this context, it is worth noting the crucial place of the State of Israel within the agenda for continuing Jewish-Catholic dialogue. Burrell's critical comments contrast sharply, for example, with Flannery's strong endorsement of the State. Yet both, in their extremism, show the unresolved theological problems represented by the present reality of Israel. That unresolved tension finds its way into the Vatican "Notes" and remains a vital area for our discussion and debate.

But Abraham Peck urges that Catholics understand the outrage within the Jewish community over the appearance of the "Notes." Jews within the dialogue assert themselves principally over two critical issues: the Holocaust and the State of Israel. Here the "Notes" fail abysmally; here the agenda of Jews and Catholics is furthest apart.

First, Peck finds the "Notes" admonition that "Catechesis should . . . help in understanding the meaning *for the Jews* of the extermination during the years 1939–1945, and its consequences" ("Notes," para. 25; emphasis added) an insult both to Jews and Christians:

> Christians as well as Jews are faced today with the recognition that the Holocaust made a mockery of all our moral values. . . . And you must explain to me how we can speak about an authentic Christianity or an authentic Christian

until Christians understand that the Holocaust was a "Christian" catastrophe.

Such statements are provocative; yet they do not tell the entire story. In the minds of Jews, the State of Israel forms a counterpart to the Holocaust; Israel is the visible symbol of safety and the redemption from that evil. Peck warns that Christians must see the State of Israel not only in political and theological dimensions, but also in human terms. "Without Israel," he asserts, "we remain the 'wandering Jew,' eternally powerless, condemned to wander for our supposed sins."

These two issues loom large in Peck's vision of the future dialogue. Both Jews and Christians must strive for deeper exchange and understanding on these two points.

A way forward in the dialogue is suggested by Deborah McCauley in a paper entitled *"Nostra Aetate* and the New Jewish-Christian Feminist Dialogue." McCauley notes that Jewish and Christian dialogue has much to gain from an appreciation of the feminist critique of patriarchal religions. In particular, such understanding would help to prevent three troublesome approaches, familiar to feminists, from controlling our dialogue: triumphalism, typology, and conservative theology.

In each case, McCauley shows how feminist understanding and scholarship regarding such issues can illuminate the position in which Jews find themselves. A single example suffices to make her point:

> The Church's recent statements on women over the past decade have little to do with how women see themselves and their relationship to God, and everything to do with how the Church fits women and women's religious self-understanding into traditional Catholic teaching about women and women's "role" in the Church. . . .
>
> [In a similar manner, the 1985] "Notes" do not try to understand the Jew "as he is," nor do the "Notes" present Jews'

self-definitions "in the light of their own religious experience." Instead, the "Notes" are a document which shows
how to fit Jews and Judaism into Catholic teaching. . . . The
document is a portrait of Judaism's "role" in the Church.

The parallel McCauley perceives is striking. Equally
important is her implicit argument that what separates
Jews from Catholics also separates Catholic [and Jewish]
men from women. And this may provide a common
ground for dialogue into the next twenty years. Triumphalism is not only a problem of Jewish and Catholic
relations, but also a problem of the relationships between
men and women within the Church and Synagogue.
Perhaps by establishing this as one important point of
our shared agenda, Jews and Christians may be led
through an ominous impasse.

I

The Documents of Dialogue

This section includes the three official documents that have set the tone for improved Jewish-Catholic relations in the last two decades.

NOSTRA AETATE

The basic document of Jewish-Catholic relations, *Nostra Aetate: Declaration on the Relationship of the Church to Non-Christian Religions,* is a product of the Second Vatican Council's deliberation and was promulgated with the Pope's full authority on October 28, 1965. This document, especially its paragraph four on relations with Jews and Judaism, remains the measuring stick for current theological and practical reflection. As the papers contained in this book indicate, much of the current theological debate about Jewish-Christian relations continues to revolve around this Vatican statement.

Nearly a decade after the publication of *Nostra Aetate,* the Vatican formed a Commission for Religious Relations with the Jews (joined to the body that drafted *Nostra*

Aetate, the Secretariat for Promoting Christian Unity). As a part of its continuing reflection upon Jewish-Catholic relations, this Commission has issued two major texts that constitute commentaries on the intent and practical application of *Nostra Aetate.* These documents, issued approximately on the tenth and twentieth anniversaries of *Nostra Aetate,* form codicils to that declaration in that they spell out the fruit of recent Catholic deliberation.

THE 1975 "GUIDELINES"

The "Guidelines and Suggestions for Jewish-Catholic Relations," promulgated December 1, 1974, are careful to refer

> the reader back to [*Nostra Aetate*]. . . . On the practical level in particular, Christians must . . . strive to acquire a better knowledge . . . of the religious traditions of Judaism. . . .

> With due respect for such matters of principle, [the "Guidelines"] simply propose some essential areas of the Church's life, with a view to launching or developing sound relations between Catholics and their Jewish brothers.

The "Guidelines" thus are meant to be explanative of (and subordinate to) the Vatican II "Declaration on the Relationship of the Church to Non-Christian Religions." They make concrete suggestions in four areas: (1) dialogue, (2) liturgy, (3) teaching and education, and (4) joint social action.

In retrospect, the "Guidelines" most significant contribution was to lay out ground rules for interreligious dialogue. The "Guidelines" urged Catholics to learn which characteristics Jews deem definitive of their own religious experience, to overcome prejudice through openness of spirit, and to guarantee religious liberty and freedom from coercion (in line with the Declaration *Dignitatis Humanae*).

THE 1985 "NOTES"

As part of the Church's recent retrospective on the two decades since Vatican II, the same Vatican Commission for Religious Relations with the Jews published on June 24, 1985, its "Notes on the Correct Way to Present Jews and Judaism in Preaching and Catechesis in the Roman Catholic Church." Like the "Guidelines," the "Notes" are meant to lay forth a proper understanding and implementation of *Nostra Aetate*, especially as that document affects teaching and education.

Six parts comprise the "Notes": (1) religious teaching and Judaism, (2) relations between the Old and New Testaments, (3) the Jewish roots of Christianity, (4) the Jews in the New Testament, (5) liturgy, and (6) Judaism and Christianity in history.

This twentieth anniversary document aims to remedy

a painful ignorance of the history and traditions of Judaism, of which only negative aspects and often caricature seem to form part of the stock ideas of many Christians.

The "Notes'" strength lies in their careful and scholarly assessment of the historical links between earliest Christianity and its Jewish environment. Hence the "Notes" clarify Jesus' relationship to other Jewish groups of his time, most notably the Pharisees, and they indicate the polemical character of the New Testament record.

At the same time, however, the "Notes" have been proclaimed by the International Jewish Committee on Interreligious Consultation to be "a retreat from earlier Catholic statements," especially with regard to two issues: the place of the Holocaust within Catholic theology and the proper attitude toward the State of Israel. Precisely these two issues loom large in the theological reflections included here, a clear indication that, for all the gains of the last twenty years, significant thought about Jewish-Catholic relations remains in its infancy.

1. Declaration on the Relationship of the Church to Non-Christian Religions

Paul, Bishop
Servant of the Servants of God
Together with the Fathers of the Sacred Council
For Everlasting Memory

1. In our times, when every day men are being drawn closer together and the ties between various peoples are being multiplied, the Church is giving deeper study to her relationship with non-Christian religions. In her task of fostering unity and love among men, and even among nations, she gives primary consideration in this document to what human beings have in common and to what promotes fellowship among them.

For all peoples comprise a single community, and have a single origin, since God made the whole race of men dwell over the entire face of the earth (cf. Acts 17:26). One also is their final goal: God. His providence, His manifestations of goodness, and His saving designs extend to all men (cf. Wisd. of Sol. 8:1; Acts 14:17; Rom. 2:6–7; 1 Tim. 2:4) against the day when the elect will be united in that Holy City ablaze with the splendor of God, where the nations will walk in His light (cf. Rev. 21:23 f.).

Men look to the various religions for answers to those profound mysteries of the human condition which, today even as in olden times, deeply stir the human heart:

What is a man? What is the meaning and the purpose of our life? What is goodness and what is sin? What gives rise to our sorrows and to what intent? Where lies the path to true happiness? What is the truth about death, judgment, and retribution beyond the grave? What, finally, is that ultimate and unutterable mystery which engulfs our being, and whence we take our rise, and whither our journey leads us?

2. From ancient times down to the present, there has existed among diverse peoples a certain perception of that hidden power which hovers over the course of things and over the events of human life; at times, indeed, recognition can be found of a supreme divinity and of a supreme father too. Such a perception and such a recognition instill the lives of these peoples with a profound religious sense. Religions bound up with cultural advancement have struggled to reply to these same questions with more refined concepts and in more highly developed language.

Thus in Hinduism men contemplate the divine mystery and express it through an unspent fruitfulness of myths and through searching philosophical inquiry. They seek release from the anguish of our condition through ascetical practices or deep meditation or a loving, trusting flight toward God.

Buddhism in its multiple forms acknowledges the radical insufficiency of this shifting world. It teaches a path by which men, in a devout and confident spirit, can either reach a state of absolute freedom or attain supreme enlightenment by their own efforts or by higher assistance.

Likewise, other religions to be found everywhere strive variously to answer the restless searchings of the human heart by proposing "ways," which consist of teachings, rules of life, and sacred ceremonies.

The Catholic Church rejects nothing which is true and

holy in these religions. She looks with sincere respect upon those ways of conduct and of life, those rules and teachings which, though differing in many particulars from what she holds and sets forth, nevertheless often reflect a ray of that truth which enlightens all men. Indeed, she proclaims and must ever proclaim Christ, "the way, the truth, and the life" (John 14:6), in whom men find the fullness of religious life, and in whom God has reconciled all things to Himself (cf. 2 Cor. 5:18–19).

The Church therefore has this exhortation for her sons: prudently and lovingly, through dialogue and collaboration with the followers of other religions, and in witness of Christian faith and life, acknowledge, preserve, and promote the spiritual and moral goods found among these men, as well as the values in their society and culture.

3. Upon the Moslems, too, the Church looks with esteem. They adore one God, living and enduring, merciful and all-powerful, maker of heaven and earth and speaker to men. They strive to submit wholeheartedly even to His inscrutable decrees, just as did Abraham, with whom the Islamic faith is pleased to associate itself. Though they do not acknowledge Jesus as God, they revere Him as a prophet. They also honor Mary, His virgin mother; at times they call on her, too, with devotion. In addition they await the day of judgment when God will give each man his due after raising him up. Consequently, they prize the moral life, and give worship to God especially through prayer, almsgiving, and fasting.

Although in the course of the centuries many quarrels and hostilities have arisen between Christians and Moslems, this most sacred Synod urges all to forget the past to strive sincerely for mutual understanding. On behalf of all mankind, let them make common cause of safeguarding and fostering social justice, moral values, peace, and freedom.

4. As this sacred Synod searches into the mystery of the Church, it recalls the spiritual bond linking the people of the new covenant with Abraham's stock.

For the Church of Christ acknowledges that, according to the mystery of God's saving design, the beginnings of her faith and her election are already found among the patriarchs, Moses, and the prophets. She professes that all who believe in Christ, Abraham's sons according to faith (cf. Gal. 3:7), are included in the same patriarch's call, and likewise that the salvation of the Church was mystically foreshadowed by the chosen people's exodus from the land of bondage.

The Church, therefore, cannot forget that she received the revelation of the Old Testament through the people with whom God in his inexpressible mercy deigned to establish the ancient covenant. Nor can she forget that she draws sustenance from the root of that good olive tree onto which have been grafted the wild olive branches of the gentiles (cf. Rom. 11:17–24). Indeed, the Church believes that by His cross Christ, our peace, reconciled Jew and Gentile, making them both one in Himself (cf. Eph. 2:14–16).

Also, the Church ever keeps in mind the words of the apostle about his kinsmen, "who have the adoption as sons, and the glory and the covenant and the legislation and the worship and the promises; who have the fathers, and from whom is Christ according to the flesh" (Rom. 9:4–5), the son of the virgin Mary. The Church recalls too that from the Jewish people sprang the apostles, her foundation stones and pillars, as well as most of the early disciples who proclaimed Christ to the world.

As holy Scripture testifies, Jerusalem did not recognize the time of her visitation (cf. Luke 19:44), nor did the Jews in large number accept the gospel; indeed, not a few opposed the spreading of it (cf. Rom. 11:28). Nevertheless, according to the apostle, the Jews still remain most dear to God because of their fathers, for He does not repent of the gifts He makes nor of the calls He issues (cf. Rom. 11:28–29). In company with the prophets and the same apostle, the Church awaits that day, known to God alone, on which all peoples will address the Lord in a single voice and "serve him with one accord" (Zeph. 3:9; cf. Isa. 66:23; Ps. 65:4; Rom. 11:11–32).

Since the spiritual patrimony common to Christians and Jews is thus so great, this sacred Synod wishes to foster and recommend that mutual understanding and respect which is the fruit above all of biblical and theological studies, and of brotherly dialogues.

True, authorities of the Jews and those who followed their lead pressed for the death of Christ (cf. John 19:6); still, what happened in His passion cannot be blamed upon all the Jews then living, without distinction, nor upon the Jews of today. Although the Church is the new people of God, the Jews should not be presented as repudiated or cursed by God, as if such views followed from the holy Scriptures. All should take pains, then, lest in catechetical instruction and in the preaching of God's Word they teach anything out of harmony with the truth of the gospel and the spirit of Christ.

The Church repudiates all persecutions against any man. Moreover, mindful of her common patrimony with the Jews, and motivated by the gospel's spiritual love and by no political considerations, she deplores the hatred, persecutions, and displays of anti-Semitism directed against the Jews at any time and from any source.

Besides, as the Church has always held and continues to hold, Christ in His boundless love freely underwent His passion and death because of the sins of all men, so that all might attain salvation. It is, therefore, the duty of the Church's preaching to proclaim the cross of Christ as the sign of God's all-embracing love and as the fountain from which every grace flows.

5. We cannot in truthfulness call upon that God who is the father of all if we refuse to act in a brotherly way toward certain men, created though they be to God's image. A man's relationship with God the Father and his relationship with his brother men are so linked together that Scripture says: "He who does not love does not know God" (1 John 4:8).

The ground is therefore removed from every theory or practice which leads to a distinction between men or peoples in the matter of human dignity and the rights which flow from it.

As a consequence, the Church rejects, as foreign to the mind of Christ, any discrimination against men or harassment of them because of their race, color, condition of life, or religion.

Accordingly, following in the footsteps of the holy apostles Peter and Paul, this sacred Synod ardently implores the Christian faithful to "maintain good fellowship among the nations" (1 Pet. 2:12), and, if possible, as far as in them lies, to keep peace with all men (cf. Rom. 12:18), so that they may truly be sons of the father who is in heaven (cf. Matt. 5:45).

Each and every one of the things set forth in this Declaration has won the consent of the fathers of this most sacred Council. We too, by the apostolic authority conferred on us by Christ, join with the venerable fathers in approving, decreeing, and establishing these things in the Holy Spirit, and we direct that what has thus been enacted in synod be published to God's glory.

Rome, at St. Peter's, October 28, 1965
I, Paul, Bishop of the Catholic Church

2. Guidelines and Suggestions for Jewish-Christian Relations

The declaration *Nostra Aetate,* issued by the Second Vatican Council on October 28, 1965, "on the relationship of the Church to non-Christian religions" (n.4), marks an important milestone in the history of Jewish-Christian relations.

Moreover, the step taken by the council finds its historical setting in circumstances deeply affected by the memory of the persecution and massacre of Jews which took place in Europe just before and during the Second World War.

Although Christianity sprang from Judaism, taking from it certain essential elements of its faith and divine cult, the gap dividing them was deepened more and more, to such an extent that Christian and Jew hardly knew each other.

After two thousand years, too often marked by mutual ignorance and frequent confrontation, the declaration *Nostra Aetate* provides an opportunity to open or to continue a dialogue with a view to better mutual understanding. Over the past nine years, many steps in this direction have been taken in various countries. As a result, it is easier to distinguish the conditions under which a new relationship between Jews and Christians may be worked out and developed.

This seems the right moment to propose, following the guidelines of the council, some concrete suggestions born of experience, hoping that they will help to bring into actual existence in the life of the Church the intentions expressed in the conciliar document.

While referring the reader back to this document, we may simply restate here that the spiritual bonds and historical links binding the Church to Judaism condemn (as opposed to the very spirit of Christianity) all forms of anti-Semitism and discrimination, which in any case the dignity of the human person alone would suffice to condemn. Further still, these links and relationships render obligatory a better mutual understanding and renewed mutual esteem. On the practical level in particular, Christians must therefore strive to acquire a better knowledge of the basic components of the religious tradition of Judaism; they must strive to learn by what essential traits the Jews define themselves in the light of their own religious experience.

With due respect for such matters of principle, we simply propose some first practical applications in different essential areas of the Church's life, with a view to launching or developing sound relations between Catholics and their Jewish brothers.

I. DIALOGUE

To tell the truth, such relations as there have been between Jew and Christian have scarcely ever risen above the level of monologue. From now on, real dialogue must be established.

Dialogue presupposes that each side wishes to know the other, and wishes to increase and deepen its knowledge of the other. It constitutes a particularly suitable means of favoring a better mutual knowledge and, especially in the case of dialogue between Jews and Christians, of probing the riches of one's own tradition. Dialogue demands respect for the other as he is; above all, respect for his faith and his religious convictions.

In virtue of her divine mission, and her very nature, the Church must preach Jesus Christ to the world (*Ad Gentes,* 2). Lest the witness of Catholics to Jesus Christ should give offence to Jews, they must take care to live and spread their Christian faith while maintaining the strictest respect for religious liberty in line with the teaching of the Second Vatican Council (Declaration *Dignitatis Humanae*). They will likewise strive to understand the difficulties which arise for the Jewish soul—rightly imbued with an extremely high, pure notion of the divine transcendence—when faced with the mystery of the incarnate Word.

While it is true that a widespread air of suspicion, inspired by an unfortunate past, is still dominant in this particular area, Christians, for their part, will be able to see to what extent the responsibility is theirs and deduce practical conclusions for the future.

In addition to friendly talks, competent people will be encouraged to meet and to study together the many problems deriving from the fundamental convictions of Judaism and of Christianity. In order not to hurt (even involuntarily) those taking part, it will be vital to guarantee, not only tact, but a great openness of spirit and diffidence with respect to one's own prejudices.

In whatever circumstances as shall prove possible and mutually acceptable, one might encourage a common meeting in the presence of God, in prayer and silent meditation, a highly efficacious way of finding that humility, that openness of heart and mind, necessary prerequisites for a deep knowledge of oneself and of others. In particular, that will be done in connection with great causes such as the struggle for peace and justice.

II. LITURGY

The existing links between the Christian liturgy and the Jewish liturgy will be borne in mind. The idea of a living community in the service of God, and in the service of men for the love of God, such as it is realized in the liturgy, is just as characteristic of the Jewish liturgy as it is of the Christian one. To improve Jewish-Christian relations, it is important to take cognizance of those common elements of the liturgical life (formulas, feasts, rites, etc.) in which the Bible holds an essential place.

An effort will be made to acquire a better understanding of whatever in the Old Testament retains its own perpetual value (cf. *Dei Verbum*, 14–15), since that has not been cancelled by the later interpretation of the New Testament. Rather, the New Testament brings out the full meaning of the Old, while both Old and New illumine and explain each other (cf. ibid., 16). This is all the more important since liturgical reform is now bringing the text of the Old Testament ever more frequently to the attention of Christians.

When commenting on biblical texts, emphasis will be laid on the continuity of our faith with that of the earlier covenant, in the perspective of the promises, without minimizing those elements of Christianity which are original. We believe that those promises were fulfilled with the first coming of Christ. But it is nonetheless true that we still await their perfect fulfillment in His glorious return at the end of time.

With respect to liturgical readings, care will be taken to see that homilies based on them will not distort their meaning, especially when it is a question of passages which seem to show the Jewish people as such in an unfavorable light. Efforts will be made so to instruct the Christian people that they will understand the true interpretation of all the texts and their meaning for the contemporary believer.

Commissions entrusted with the task of liturgical translation will pay particular attention to the way in which they express those phrases and passages which Christians, if not well informed, might misunderstand because of prejudice. Obviously, one cannot alter the text of the Bible. The point is that, with a version destined for liturgical use, there should be an overriding preoccupation to bring out explicitly the meaning of a text, while taking scriptural studies into account.

The preceding remarks also apply to introductions to biblical readings, to the prayer of the faithful, and to commentaries printed in missals used by the laity.

III. TEACHING AND EDUCATION

Although there is still a great deal of work to be done, a better understanding of Judaism itself and its relationship to Christianity has been achieved in recent years thanks to the teaching of the Church, the study and research of scholars, as also to the beginning of dialogue. In this respect, the following facts deserve to be recalled.

—It is the same God, "inspirer and author of the books of both Testaments" (*Dei Verbum*, 16), who speaks both in the old and new covenants.

—Judaism in the time of Christ and the apostles was a complex reality embracing many different trends, many spiritual, religious, social and cultural values.

—The Old Testament and the Jewish tradition founded upon it must not be set against the New Testament in such a way that the former seems to constitute a religion of only justice, fear, and legalism, with no appeal to the love of God and neighbor (cf. Deut. 6:5, Lev. 19:18, Matt. 22:34–40).

—Jesus was born of the Jewish people, as were his apostles and a large number of his first disciples. When he revealed himself as the Messiah and Son of God (cf.

Matt. 16:16), the bearer of the new gospel message, he did so as the fulfillment and perfection of the earlier revelation. And, although his teaching had a profoundly new character, Christ, nevertheless, in many instances, took his stand on the teaching of the Old Testament. The New Testament is profoundly marked by its relation to the Old. As the Second Vatican Council declared: "God, the inspirer and author of the books of both Testaments, wisely arranged that the New Testament be hidden in the Old and the Old be made manifest in the New" (*Dei Verbum*, 16). Jesus also used teaching methods similar to those employed by the rabbis of his time.

—With regard to the trial and death of Jesus, the council recalled that "what happened in his passion cannot be blamed upon all the Jews then living, without distinction, nor upon the Jews of today" (*Nostra Aetate*, 4).[1]

—The history of Judaism did not end with the destruction of Jerusalem, but rather went on to develop a religious tradition. And, although we believe that the importance and meaning of that tradition were deeply affected by the coming of Christ, it is still nonetheless rich in religious values.

—With the prophets and the apostle Paul, "the church awaits the day, known to God alone, on which all peoples will address the Lord in a single voice and 'serve him with one accord' (Zeph. 3:9)" (*Nostra Aetate*, 4).

Information concerning these questions is important at all levels of Christian instruction and education. Among sources of information, special attention should be paid to the following:

—catechisms and religious textbooks
—history books
—the mass-media (press, radio, cinema, television).

The effective use of these means presupposes the thorough formation of instructors and educators in training schools, seminaries, and universities.

Research into the problems bearing on Judaism and Jewish-Christian relations will be encouraged among specialists, particularly in the fields of exegesis, theology, history, and sociology. Higher institutions of Catholic research, in association if possible with other similar Christian institutions and experts, are invited to contribute to the solution of such problems. Wherever possible, chairs of Jewish studies will be created, and collaboration with Jewish scholars encouraged.

IV. JOINT SOCIAL ACTION

Jewish and Christian tradition, founded on the word of God, is aware of the value of the human person, the image of God. Love of the same God must show itself in effective action for the good of mankind. In the spirit of the prophets, Jews and Christians will work willingly together, seeking social justice and peace at every level—local, national and international.

At the same time, such collaboration can do much to foster mutual understanding and esteem.

CONCLUSION

The Second Vatican Council has pointed out the path to follow in promoting deep fellowship between Jews and Christians. But there is still a long road ahead.

The problem of Jewish-Christian relations concerns the Church as such since it is when "pondering her own mystery" that she encounters the mystery of Israel. Therefore, even in areas where no Jewish communities exist, this remains an important problem. There is also an ecumenical aspect to the question: the very return of Christians to the sources and origins of their faith, grafted on to the earlier covenant, helps the search for unity in Christ, the cornerstone.

In this field, the bishops will know what best to do on the pastoral level, within the general disciplinary framework of the Church and in line with the common teaching of her magisterium. For example, they will create some suitable commissions or secretariats on a national or regional level, or appoint some competent person to promote the implementation of the conciliar directives and the suggestions made above.

On October 22, 1974, the Holy Father instituted for the universal Church this Commission for Religious Relations with the Jews, joined to the Secretariat for Promoting Christian Unity. This special commission, created to encourage and foster religious relations between Jews and Catholics—and to do so eventually in collaboration with other Christians—will be, within the limits of its competence, at the service of all interested organizations, providing information for them, and helping them to pursue their task in conformity with the instructions of the Holy See.

The commission wishes to develop this collaboration in order to implement, correctly and effectively, the express intentions of the council.

NOTES

1. Thus the formula "the Jews," in St. John, sometimes according to the context means "the leaders of the Jews," or "the adversaries of Jesus," terms which express better the thought of the evangelist and avoid appearing to arraign the Jewish people as such. Another example is the use of the words "pharisee" and "pharisaism" which have taken a largely pejorative meaning.

3. Notes on the Correct Way to Present Jews and Judaism in Preaching and Catechesis in the Roman Catholic Church

On March 6, 1982, Pope John Paul II told delegates of episcopal conferences and other experts meeting in Rome to study relations between the Church and Judaism:

> You yourselves were concerned during your sessions with Catholic teaching and catechesis regarding Jews and Judaism . . . We should aim, in this field, that Catholic teaching at its different levels, in catechesis to children and young people, presents Jews and Judaism not only in an honest and objective manner, free from prejudices and without any offences, but also with full awareness of the heritage common to Jews and Christians.

In this passage, so charged with meaning, the Holy Father plainly drew inspiration from the council declaration *Nostra Aetate*, No. 4, which says, "All should take pains, then, lest in catechetical instruction and in the preaching of God's word they teach anything out of harmony with the truth of the Gospel and the spirit of Christ"; as also from these words: "Since the spiritual patrimony common to Christians and Jews is thus so great, this sacred synod wishes to foster and recommend mutual understanding and respect."

31

In the same way, the "Guidelines and Suggestions for Jewish-Christian Relations" ends its Chapter 3, titled "Teaching and Education," which lists a number of practical things to be done, with this recommendation:

> Information concerning these questions is important at all levels of Christian instruction and education. Among sources of information, special attention should be paid the following:
> —catechisms and religious textbooks;
> —history books;
> —the mass media (press, radio, cinema, television).

> The effective use of these means presupposes the thorough formation of instructors and educators in training schools, seminaries and universities (cf. AAS 77, 1975, p. 73).

The paragraphs which follow are intended to serve this purpose.

I. RELIGIOUS TEACHING AND JUDAISM

1. In *Nostra Aetate* No. 4, the council speaks of the "spiritual bonds linking" Jews and Christians and of the "great spiritual patrimony" common to both, and it further asserts that "the church of Christ acknowledges that, according to the mystery of God's saving design, the beginning of her faith and her election are already found among the patriarchs, Moses, and the prophets."
2. Because of the unique relations that exist between Christianity and Judaism—"linked together at the very level of their identity" (John Paul II, March 6, 1982)—relations "founded on the design of the God of the covenant" (ibid.), the Jews and Judaism should not occupy an occasional and marginal place in catechesis: their presence there is essential and should be organically integrated.

3. This concern for Judaism in Catholic teaching has not merely a historical or archeological foundation. As the Holy Father said in the speech already quoted, after he had again mentioned the "common patrimony" of the Church and Judaism as "considerable": "To assess it carefully in itself and with due awareness of the faith and religious life of the Jewish people *as they are professed and practiced still today,* can greatly help us to understand better certain aspects of the life of the Church." It is a question then of *pastoral* concern for a still living reality closely related to the Church. The Holy Father has stated this permanent reality of the Jewish people in a remarkable theological formula in his allocution to the Jewish community of West Germany at Mainz, November 17, 1980: "The people of God of the Old Covenant, which has never been revoked."

4. Here we should recall the passage in which the "Guidelines" (I) tried to define the fundamental condition of dialogue: "respect for the other as he is," knowledge of the "basic components of the religious tradition of Judaism" and again learning "by what essential traits the Jews define themselves in the light of their own religious experience" (Introduction).

5. The singular character and the difficulty of Christian teaching about Jews and Judaism lies in this, that it needs to balance a number of pairs of ideas which express the relation between the two economies of the Old and New Testaments:

—promise and fulfillment;
—continuity and newness;
—singularity and universality;
—uniqueness and exemplary nature.

This means that the theologian and the catechist who deals with the subject needs to show in his practice of teaching that:

—Promise and fulfillment throw light on each other.

—Newness lies in a metamorphosis of what was there before.

—The singularity of the people of the Old Testament is not exclusive and is open, in the divine vision, to a universal extension.

—The uniqueness of the Jewish people is meant to have the force of an example.

6. Finally, "work that is of poor quality and lacking in precision would be extremely detrimental" to Judeo-Christian dialogue (John Paul II, speech of March 6, 1982). But it would be above all detrimental—since we are talking of teaching and education—to Christian identity (ibid.).

7. "In virtue of her divine mission, the Church," which is to be "the all-embracing means of salvation" in which alone "the fullness of the means of salvation can be obtained" (*Unitatis Redintegratio*, 3), "must of her nature proclaim Jesus Christ to the world" (cf. "Guidelines" I). Indeed, we believe that it is through him that we go to the Father (cf. John 14:6) and, "Eternal life is this: to know you, the only true God, and Him whom you have sent, Jesus Christ" (John 17:3).

Jesus affirms (John 10:16) that "there shall be one flock and one shepherd." Church and Judaism cannot then be seen as two parallel ways of salvation and the Church must witness to Christ as the redeemer for all, "while maintaining the strictest respect for religious liberty in line with the teaching of the Second Vatican Council" (*Dignitatis Humanae*; cf. "Guidelines" I).

8. The urgency and importance of precise, objective, and rigorously accurate teaching on Judaism for our faithful follows too from the danger of anti-Semitism which is always ready to reappear under different guises. The question is not merely to uproot from among the faithful the remains of anti-Semitism still to be found here and there, but much rather to arouse in them,

through educational work, an exact knowledge of the wholly unique "bond" (*Nostra Aetate*, 4) which joins us as a church to the Jews and to Judaism. In this way, they would learn to appreciate and love the latter, who have been chosen by God to prepare the coming of Christ and have preserved everything that was progressively revealed and given in the course of that preparation, notwithstanding their difficulty in recognizing in him their Messiah.

II. RELATIONS BETWEEN THE OLD AND NEW TESTAMENTS[1]

1. Our aim should be to show the unity of biblical revelation (Old Testament and New Testament) and of the divine plan, before speaking of each historical event, so as to stress that particular events have meaning when seen in history as a whole—from creation to fulfillment. This history concerns the whole human race and especially believers. Thus the definitive meaning of the election of Israel does not become clear except in the light of the complete fulfillment (Rom. 9–11), and election in Jesus Christ is still better understood with reference to the announcement and the promise (cf. Heb. 4:1–11).

2. We are dealing with singular happenings which concern a singular nation but are destined, in the sight of God who reveals his purpose, to take on universal and exemplary significance.

The aim is moreover to present the events of the Old Testament not as concerning only the Jews but also as touching us personally. Abraham is truly the father of our faith (cf. Rom. 4:11–12; Roman Canon: *patriarchae nostri Abrahae*). And it is said (1 Cor. 10:1): "Our fathers were all under the cloud, and all passed through the sea." The patriarchs, prophets, and other personalities of the

Old Testament have been venerated and always will be venerated as saints in the liturgical tradition of the Oriental church as also of the Latin church.

3. From the unity of the divine plan derives the problem of the relation between the Old and New Testaments. The Church already from apostolic times (cf. 1 Cor. 10:11; Heb. 10:1) and then constantly in tradition resolved this problem by means of typology, which emphasizes the primordial value that the Old Testament must have in the Christian view. Typology, however, makes many people uneasy and is perhaps the sign of a problem unresolved.

4. Hence in using typology, the teaching and practice of which we have received from the liturgy and from the fathers of the Church, we should be careful to avoid any transition from the Old to the New Testament which might seem merely a rupture. The Church, in the spontaneity of the Spirit which animates her, has vigorously condemned the attitude of Marcion[2] and always opposed his dualism.

5. It should also be emphasized that typological interpretation consists in reading the Old Testament as preparation and, in certain aspects, outline and foreshadowing of the New (cf. e.g., Heb. 5:5–10, etc.). Christ is henceforth the key and point of reference to the Scriptures: "The rock was Christ" (1 Cor. 10:4).

6. It is true then, and should be stressed, that the Church and Christians read the Old Testament in the light of the event of the dead and risen Christ and that on these grounds there is a Christian reading of the Old Testament which does not necessarily coincide with the Jewish reading. Thus Christian identity and Jewish identity should be carefully distinguished in their respective reading of the Bible. But this detracts nothing from the value of the Old Testament in the Church and does nothing to hinder Christians from profiting discerningly from the traditions of Jewish reading.

7. Typological reading only manifests the unfathomable riches of the Old Testament, its inexhaustible content and the mystery of which it is full, and should not lead us to forget that it retains its own value as revelation that the New Testament often does no more than resume (cf. Mark 12:29–31). Moreover, the New Testament itself demands to be read in the light of the Old. Primitive Christian catechesis constantly had recourse to this (cf. e.g., 1 Cor. 5:6–8; 10:1–11).

8. Typology further signifies reaching toward the accomplishment of the divine plan, when "God will be all in all" (1 Cor. 15:28). This holds true also for the Church which, realized already in Christ, yet awaits its definitive perfecting as the body of Christ. The fact that the body of Christ is still tending toward its full stature (cf. Eph. 4:12–19) takes nothing from the value of being a Christian. So also the calling of the patriarchs and the exodus from Egypt do not lose their importance and value in God's design from being at the same time intermediate stages (cf. e.g., *Nostra Aetate*, 4).

9. The exodus, for example, represents an experience of salvation and liberation that is not complete in itself, but has in it, over and above its own meaning, the capacity to be developed further. Salvation and liberation are already accomplished in Christ and gradually realized by the sacraments in the Church. This makes way for the fulfillment of God's design, which awaits its final consummation with the return of Jesus as Messiah, for which we pray each day. The kingdom, for the coming of which we also pray each day, will be finally established. With salvation and liberation the elect and the whole of creation will be transformed in Christ (Rom. 8:19–23).

10. Furthermore, in underlining the eschatological dimension of Christianity we shall reach a greater awareness that the people of God of the Old and the New Testaments are tending toward a like end in the future: the coming or return of the Messiah—even if they start

from two different points of view. It is more clearly understood that the person of the Messiah is not only a point of division for the people of God but also a point of convergence (cf. *Sussidi per l'ecumenismo* of the Diocese of Rome, No. 140). Thus it can be said that Jews and Christians meet in a comparable hope, founded on the same promise made to Abraham (cf. Gen. 12:1–3; Heb. 6:13–18).

11. Attentive to the same God who has spoken, hanging on the same word, we have to witness to one same memory and one common hope in him who is the master of history. We must also accept our responsibility to prepare the world for the coming of the Messiah by working together for social justice, respect for the rights of persons and nations and for social and international reconciliation. To this we are driven, Jews and Christians, by the command to love our neighbor, by a common hope for the kingdom of God, and by the great heritage of the prophets. Transmitted soon enough by catechesis, such a conception would teach young Christians in a practical way to cooperate with Jews, going beyond simple dialogue (cf. "Guidelines," IV).

III. JEWISH ROOTS OF CHRISTIANITY

12. Jesus was and always remained a Jew, his ministry was deliberately limited "to the lost sheep of the house of Israel" (Matt. 15:24). Jesus was fully a man of his time and of his environment—the Jewish Palestinian one of the first century, the anxieties and hopes of which he shared. This cannot but underline both the reality of the incarnation and the very meaning of the history of salvation, as it has been revealed in the Bible (cf. Rom. 1:3–4; Gal. 4:4–5).

13. Jesus' relations with biblical law and its more or less traditional interpretations are undoubtedly complex and

he showed great liberty toward it (cf. the "antitheses" of the Sermon on the Mount: Matt. 5:21–48, bearing in mind the exegetical difficulties; his attitude to rigorous observance of the Sabbath: Mark 3:1–6, etc.)

But there is no doubt that he wished to submit himself to the law (cf. Gal. 4:4), that he was circumcised and presented in the Temple like any Jew of his time (cf. Luke 2:21, 22–24), that he was trained in the law's observance. He extolled respect for it (cf. Matt. 5:17–20) and invited obedience to it (cf. Matt. 8:4). The rhythm of his life was marked by observance of pilgrimages on great feasts, even from his infancy (cf. Luke 2:41–50; John 2:13, 7:10, etc). The importance of the cycle of the Jewish feasts has been frequently underlined in the Gospel of John (cf. John 2:13, 5:1, 7:2, 10:37, 10:22, 12:1, 13:1, 18:28, 19:42, etc.).

14. It should be noted also that Jesus often taught in the synagogues (cf. Matt. 4:23, 9:35; Luke 4:15–18; John 18:20, etc.) and in the Temple (cf. John 18:20, etc.), which he frequented as did the disciples even after the resurrection (cf. e.g., Acts 2:46, 3:1, 21:26, etc.). He wished to put in the context of synagogue worship the proclamation of his messiahship (cf. Luke 4:16–21). But above all he wished to achieve the supreme act of the gift of himself in the setting of the domestic liturgy of the Passover, or at least of the paschal festivity (cf. Mark 14:1, 12 and parallels; John 18:28). This also allows of a better understanding of the "memorial" character of the eucharist.

15. Thus the Son of God is incarnate in a people and a human family (cf. Gal. 4:4; Rom. 9:5). This takes away nothing, quite the contrary, from the fact that he was born for all men (Jewish shepherds and pagan wise men are found at his crib: Luke 2:8–20; Matt. 2:1–12) and died for all men (at the foot of the cross there are Jews, among them Mary and John: John 19:25–27, and pagans like the centurion; Mark 15:39 and parallels).

Thus he made two peoples one in his flesh (cf. Eph.

2:14–17). This explains why with the *ecclesia ex gentibus* we have, in Palestine and elsewhere, an *ecclesia ex circumcisione,* of which Eusebius, for example, speaks (H.E. IV, 5).

16. His relations with the Pharisees were not always or wholly polemical. Of this there are many proofs:

—It is Pharisees who warn Jesus of the risks he is running (Luke 13:31).

—Some Pharisees are praised—e.g., "the scribe" of Mark 12:34.

—Jesus eats with Pharisees (Luke 7:36, 14:1).

17. Jesus shares, with the majority of Palestinian Jews of that time, some pharisaic doctrines: the resurrection of the body; forms of piety, like almsgiving, prayer, fasting (cf. Matt. 6:1–18), and the liturgical practice of addressing God as father; the priority of the commandment to love God and our neighbor (cf. Mark 12:28–34). This is so also with Paul (cf. Acts 23:8), who always considered his membership of the Pharisees as a title of honor (cf. ibid. 23:6, 26:5; Philem. 3:5).

18. Paul also, like Jesus himself, used methods of reading and interpreting Scripture and of teaching his disciples that were common to the Pharisees of their time. This applies to the use of parables in Jesus' ministry, as also to the method of Jesus and Paul of supporting a conclusion with a quotation from Scripture.

19. It is noteworthy too that the Pharisees are not mentioned in accounts of the passion. Gamaliel (Acts 5:34–39) defends the apostles in a meeting of the Sanhedrin. An exclusively negative picture of the Pharisees is likely to be inaccurate and unjust (cf. "Guidelines," note 1; cf. AAS, loc. cit. p. 76). If in the Gospels and elsewhere in the New Testament there are all sorts of unfavorable references to the Pharisees, they should be seen against the background of a complex and diversified movement. Criticism of various types of Pharisees are moreover not lacking in rabbinical sources (cf.

Babylonian Talmud, Sotah 22b, etc.). "Phariseeism" in the pejorative sense can be rife in any religion. It may also be stressed that, if Jesus shows himself severe toward the Pharisees, it is because he is closer to them than to other contemporary Jewish groups (cf. *supra* 17).

20. All this should help us to understand better what St. Paul says (Rom. 11:16ff) about the "root" and the "branches." The Church and Christianity, for all their novelty, find their origin in the Jewish milieu of the first century of our era, and more deeply still in the "design of God" (*Nostra Aetate,* 4), realized in the patriarchs, Moses, and the prophets (ibid.), down to its consummation in Christ Jesus.

IV. THE JEWS IN THE NEW TESTAMENT

21. The "Guidelines" already say (note 1) that "the formula 'the Jews' sometimes according to the context means 'the leaders of the Jews' or 'the adversaries of Jesus,' terms which express better the thought of the evangelist and avoid appearing to arraign the Jewish people as such."

An objective presentation of the role of the Jewish people in the New Testament should take account of these various facts:

(A.) The Gospels are the outcome of long and complicated editorial work. The dogmatic constitution *Dei Verbum,* following the Pontifical Biblical Commission's instruction *Sancta Mater Ecclesia,* distinguishes three stages: "The sacred authors wrote the four Gospels, selecting some things from the many which had been handed on by word of mouth or in writing, reducing some of them to a synthesis, explicating some things in view of the situation of their churches, and preserving the form of proclamation, but always in such fashion that they told us the honest truth about Jesus" (No. 19).

Hence it cannot be ruled out that some references hostile or less than favorable to the Jews have their historical context in conflicts between the nascent church and the Jewish community. Certain controversies reflect Christian-Jewish relations long after the time of Jesus.

To establish this is of capital importance if we wish to bring out the meaning of certain gospel texts for the Christians of today.

All this should be taken into account when preparing catechesis and homilies for the last weeks of Lent and Holy Week (cf. already "Guidelines," II, and now also *Sussidi per l'ecumenismo* of the Diocese of Rome, 1982, 144b).

(B.) It is clear on the other hand that there were conflicts between Jesus and certain categories of Jews of his time, among them Pharisees, from the beginning of his ministry (cf. Mark 2:1–11, 24, 3:6, etc.).

(C.) There is moreover the sad fact that the majority of the Jewish people and its authorities did not believe in Jesus—a fact not merely of history but of theological bearing, of which St. Paul tries hard to plumb the meaning (Rom. 9–11).

(D.) This fact, accentuated as the Christian mission developed, especially among the pagans, led inevitably to a rupture between Judaism and the young church, now irreducibly separated and divergent in faith, and this stage of affairs is reflected in the texts of the New Testament and particularly in the Gospels. There is no question of playing down or glossing over this rupture; that could only prejudice the identity of either side. Nevertheless it certainly does not cancel the spiritual "bond" of which the council speaks (*Nostra Aetate*, 4) and which we propose to dwell on here.

(E.) Reflecting on this in the light of Scripture, notably of the chapters cited from the Epistle to the Romans, Christians should never forget that the faith is a free gift of God (cf. Rom. 9:12) and that we should never judge the consciences of others. St. Paul's exhoration "do not boast" in your attitude to "the root" (Rom. 11:18) has its full point here.

(F.) There is no putting the Jews who knew Jesus and did not believe in him, or those who opposed the preaching of the apostles, on the same plane with Jews who came after or those of today. If the responsibility of the former remains a mystery hidden with God (cf. Rom. 11:25), the latter are in an entirely different situation. Vatican II, in the *Declaration on Religious Liberty,* teaches that "all men are to be immune from coercion . . . in such wise that in matters religious no one is to be forced to act in a manner contrary to his own beliefs. Nor . . . restrained from acting in accordance with his own beliefs" (No. 2). This is one of the bases—proclaimed by the council—on which Judeo-Christian dialogue rests.

22. The delicate question of responsibility for the death of Christ must be looked at from the standpoint of the conciliar declaration *Nostra Aetate,* 4, and of "Guidelines," III: "What happened in [Christ's] passion cannot be blamed upon all the Jews then living without distinction nor upon the Jews of today," especially since "authorities of the Jews and those who followed their lead pressed for the death of Christ." Again, further on: "Christ in his boundless love freely underwent his passion and death because of the sins of all men, so that all might attain salvation" (*Nostra Aetate,* 4). The catechism of the Council of Trent teaches that Christian sinners are more to blame for the death of Christ than those few Jews who brought it about—they indeed "knew not what they did" (cf. Luke 23:34) and we know it only too well (Pars I, Caput V, Quaest. XI). In the same way and for the same reason, "the Jews should not be presented as repudiated or cursed by God, as if such views followed from the Holy Scriptures" (*Nostra Aetate,* 4), even though it is true that "the Church is the new people of God" (ibid).

V. THE LITURGY

23. Jews and Christians find in the Bible the very substance of their liturgy: for the proclamation of God's word, response to it, prayer of praise and intercession for the living and the dead, recourse to the divine mercy. The Liturgy of the Word in its own structure originates in Judaism. The Prayer of Hours and other liturgical texts and formularies have their parallels in Judaism as do the very formulas of our most venerable prayers, among them the Our Father. The eucharistic prayers also draw inspiration from models in the Jewish tradition. As John Paul II said (ibid.): "The faith and religious life of the Jewish people as they are professed and practiced still today can greatly help us to understand better certain aspects of the life of the Church. Such is the case of liturgy."

24. This is particularly evident in the great feasts of the liturgical year, like the Passover. Christians and Jews celebrate the Passover: the Jews, the historic Passover looking toward the future; the Christians, the Passover accomplished in the death and resurrection of Christ, although still in expectation of the final consummation (cf. *supra*, No. 9). It is still the "memorial" which comes to us from the Jewish tradition, with a specific content different in each case. On either side, however, there is a like dynamism: for Christians it gives meaning to the eucharistic celebration (cf. the antiphon *"O sacrum convivium"*), a paschal celebration and as such a making present of the past, but experienced in the expectation of what is to come.

VI. JUDAISM AND CHRISTIANITY IN HISTORY

25. The history of Israel did not end in 70 A.D. (cf. "Guidelines," II). It continued, especially in a numerous Diaspora which allowed Israel to carry to the whole world

a witness—often heroic—of its fidelity to the one God and to "exalt him in the presence of all the living" (Tob. 13:4), while preserving the memory of the land of their forefathers at the heart of their hope (Passover seder).

Christians are invited to understand this religious attachment which finds its roots in biblical tradition, without, however, making their own any particular religious interpretation of this relationship (cf. Declaration of the U.S. National Conference of Catholic Bishops, Nov. 20, 1975).

The existence of the State of Israel and its political options should be envisaged not in a perspective which is in itself religious, but in their reference to the common principles of international law.

The permanence of Israel (while so many ancient peoples have disappeared without trace) is a historic fact and a sign to be interpreted within God's design. We must in any case rid ourselves of the traditional idea of a people *punished,* preserved as a *living argument* for Christian apologetic. It remains a chosen people, "the pure olive on which were grafted the branches of the wild olive which are the gentiles" (John Paul II, ibid., alluding to Rom. 11:17–24). We must remember how much the balance of relations between Jews and Christians over two thousand years has been negative. We must remind ourselves how the permanence of Israel is accompanied by a continuous spiritual fecundity in the rabbinic period, in the Middle Ages, and in modern times, taking its start from a patrimony which we long shared, so much so that "the faith and religious life of the Jewish people as they are professed and practiced still today, can greatly help us to understand better certain aspects of the life of the Church" (John Paul II, ibid.). Catechesis should on the other hand help in understanding the meaning for the Jews of the extermination during the years 1939–1945, and its consequences.

26. Education and catechesis should concern themselves with the problem of racism, still active in different

forms of anti-Semitism. The council presented it thus: "Moreover, (the Church), mindful of her common patrimony with the Jews and motivated by the Gospel's spiritual love and by no political considerations, deplores the hatred, persecutions and displays of anti-Semitism directed against the Jews at any time and from any source" (*Nostra Aetate*, 4). The "Guidelines" comment: "The spiritual bonds and historical links binding the Church to Judaism condemn (as opposed to the very spirit of Christianity) all forms of anti-Semitism and discrimination, which in any case the dignity of the human person alone would suffice to condemn" ("Guidelines," Preamble).

CONCLUSION

27. Religious teaching, catechesis, and preaching should be a preparation not only for objectivity, justice, tolerance but also for understanding and dialogue. Our two traditions are so related that they cannot ignore each other. Mutual knowledge must be encouraged at every level. There is evident in particular a painful ignorance of the history and traditions of Judaism, of which only negative aspects and often caricature seem to form part of the stock ideas of many Christians.

That is what these notes aim to remedy. This would mean that the council text and "Guidelines" would be more easily and faithfully put into practice.

Cardinal Johannes Willebrands
President
Rev. Pierre Duprey
Vice President
Msgr. Jorge Mejia
Secretary

NOTES

1. We continue to use the expression Old Testament because it is traditional (cf. already 2 Cor. 3:14), but also because "old" does not mean "out of date" or "outworn." In any case, it is the permanent value of the Old Testament as a source of Christian revelation that is emphasized here (*Dei Verbum,* 3).

2. A man of Gnostic tendency who in the second century rejected the Old Testament and part of the New as the work of an evil God, a demiurge. The church reacted strongly against this heresy (cf. Irenaeus).

II
The History of *Nostra Aetate*

4. Holy Diplomacy:
Making the Impossible Possible

THOMAS F. STRANSKY, C.S.P.

> How in a few minutes was I to make the Pope under-
> stand that at the same time as a material ghetto, there
> had been a spiritual ghetto in which the Church gradu-
> ally enclosed old Israel? . . . that the head of the
> Church, "a voice from the summit," could show the
> good path by solemnly condemning "the teaching of
> contempt," as, in essence, anti-Christian? (Jules Isaac)

Almost twenty years ago, I offered my first post-Vatican
II reflections on the shortest of the conciliar documents,
the *Declaration on the Relationship of the Church to
Non-Christian Religions,* with special attention to its paragraph four, "On the Jews." With two decades of easy
hindsight, I still have no reason or experience to change
what I then had said:

> Through the experience of Vatican II the theologian sees
> more clearly, and believes more deeply, that the Church is a
> pilgrim Church, which stands under God's Word and there-
> fore is daily judged by it, and advances only from a knowl-
> edge more or less exact of its historical situation, from an
> understanding more or less penetrating of its tasks, and
> from a response more or less faithful to those tasks.

Then, in a more personal way, I offered that

in the genesis of no document have I experienced more deeply the interaction of God's design and the concrete historical process, the dynamism of progress yet not perfectly a successful one, the holy step forward which closes a period of history yet opens a less definite future, than in the development and final form of *Nostra Aetate*.[1]

Twenty years later, I would add that of all the sixteen promulgated documents of Vatican II, none of them so clearly reveals the exercise of what I call "holy diplomacy" than does that fourth paragraph. If in secular statecraft, diplomacy is defined as the art of the possible, then holy diplomacy goes beyond this. Holy diplomacy flows from a profound biblical and experiential conviction that our God first makes the *impossible* possible; and then God works through the likes of us, Jews and Christians, to make the possible actual.

For *Nostra Aetate*, one also can use less theological rules or images. Often during the torturous journey of that draft, the Italian proverb applied: "The Romans are the worst of organizers and the best of improvisors." At a few stages, Murphy's law was activated: If the worst can happen, it will. Or its happier corollary: If the worst can happen, count the little victories when it does not.

HOLY DIPLOMACY

Consider the beginning of the beginning. Through the 1960 spring initiatives of Cardinal Augustin Bea, the seventy-eight year-old retired rector of the Biblical Institute in Rome, another seventy-eight year-old, John XXIII, announced on June 5, 1960, his creation of the Secretariat for Promoting Christian Unity. It would become the liaison between the upcoming council and other Christian communions, and the drafter of ecumenical topics. Bea was appointed its president, and during the summer he put together his three-man staff and a commission of sixteen voting bishop-members and twenty consultors. With no agenda except the umbrella mandate of promoting the unity of Christians, Bea convoked the first meeting of this fledgling group for November 14–15, 1960.[2]

In their prior discussions, Pope John and Cardinal Bea never considered Catholic-Jewish relations. In fact, according to conversations and a written memo from Monsignor Louis Capovilla, then the Pope's private secretary and confidant, until a week after he had set up Bea's Secretariat, "it never entered Pope John XXIII's mind that the Council ought to be occupied also with the Jewish question [questions ebraica] and with anti-Semitism."[3] The Jewish theme reached the Pope's consciousness at a private audience, on June 13, with Professor Jules Isaac.

This Jewish scholar had been director of education in France, the author of French textbooks, a noted historian, and promoter of the Paris-based society of Jews and Christians, Amitie judeo-chretienne. Isaac presented to Pope John a lengthy memorandum about the history of Catholic attitudes and actions toward the Jews, especially as these were expressed in the church fathers, the liturgy, and catechisms. But at the half-hour private audience, Isaac had time only to outline his report.

After Isaac's death, his unedited memoirs were found. In them Isaac reminisced,

> How in a few minutes was I to make the Pope understand that at the same time as a material ghetto, there had been a spiritual ghetto in which the Church gradually enclosed old Israel; that there had always been a Catholic "teaching of contempt" (mépris) towards the Jews, but now that tradition faces a growing counter-pressure, a purificato in the Church,

so that between the two contrary tendencies, Catholic opinion is divided, remains wavering; that the head of the Church, a voice from the summit, could show the good path by solemnly condemning the teaching of contempt, as in essence, anti-Christian?

Towards the end of the conversation, Isaac suggested that the Pope set up a committee to study "the Jewish question." "I thought of that from the beginning of our meeting," replied Pope John, according to Isaac's memoirs, and smilingly added, "You are right in having more than hope. . . . I am the head but I must also consult. . . . [The Vatican] is not an absolute monarchy."[4] He then asked Isaac to contact Bea, with whom Isaac could discuss at length his memorandum already in the Pope's hand. Isaac did so, on June 15.

The record now is silent until three months later. On September 18, 1960, Pope John formally charged Bea's Unity Secretariat with the task of preparing a declaration dealing with the Jewish people.[5] At that November plenary meeting of the Secretariat, Bea communicated this special mandate. He added that unlike other topics, even the fact of initial discussion of what he called "the Jewish question" should be, at John XXIII's request, *sub secreto.* Indeed, these two together taught so many of us, in the words of Ecclesiastes 8:9, "the art of the timely answer from old men." Had they both already anticipated the delicate, twisted path the topic would follow over the next six years? The impossible would often seem impossible.

Before that November 1960 meeting, one of my first obediences was the perusal and collation of pro or con ecumencial "wishes and desires" (*vota et desideria*) from over 2400 of the bishops, 156 superiors general (only male) of religious communities, 62 Catholic universities, Bible institutes, and the Roman Curial Congregations. The Vatican Press had published these *sub secreto*; 9,520 pages in fifteen thick volumes. My general impression, very disheartening, was of a collection of such disparate views of what Vatican II should or could be and of how it would treat Pope John's *aggiornament,* that who and what would win out was unanswerable. As for the Jews, the material was silent, except for a plea "to condemn international freemasonry, controlled by the Jews," and a carefully worded, positive, very prophetic contribution on the avoidance of anti-Semitism from nineteen of Bea's fellow Jesuits at Rome's Biblical Institute.

NOSTRA AETATE: TOO LATE, TOO SOON

We began drafting, blessed with a healthy naivete and trust in Bea's comforting "one-step-at-a-time." By November 1961 we had drafted a first schema. We improved the draft, through the crucible of leisurely debate, at four other intermittent plenaries, in time for the council's first session in October 1962. Throughout that period, a question lurked about: Was the very theme too late or too soon? The signs were not helpful; they indicated both.

The subject, on the one hand, seemed to appear too late on the Catholic horizon—twenty years after World War II and the revelations of the Holocaust obscenity. And that satanic nightmare was a stark mirror which reflected other tragic culminations in Western history: massacres of Jews during the so-called holy march to the Holy Land (Crusades); Catholic expulsion of Jews from Spain, 1492; Cossack mass murders in Poland-Lithuania in the mid-1700s and later Tzarist pogroms; the persistent hounding by the Inquisition in Rome until the last century; denial of civil rights and imposed ghettoes by Catholic governments with Vatican concordats.

Indeed, perhaps the topic was too late. The publicity about Pope John's council, which occasioned so much hope in Catholic hearts, did not incite the same optimism within the entire Jewish community. Scholarly Jews recalled that the last General Council of the Catholic Church which had placed the Jewish theme on the agenda—in Basel, Switzerland, 1432—decreed that Jews were to have no social concourse with Christians; Jews were to wear a distinctive garb, live in separate quarters of the community, be excluded from public office and from university degrees, and forced to listen to Christian sermons. Even at the end of the First Vatican Council, 1870, the last ghetto to disappear in Europe was in Rome, but that liberation was decreed not by that Church gathering but by victorious Garibaldi's new government.

General Church councils, for the Roman Catholic, may be arenas for the working of the Holy Spirit, but for Jews, any council could be a potential threat. It could, at least theologically, reinforce what Jules Isaac called Christian *mépris* or contempt for the Jewish people.

Even the ecumenical hope which Catholic, Protestant, and Orthodox Christians saw in the upcoming council— the reconciliation of all Christians into the visible fellowship that God wishes for his one Church—increased Jewish fears. Some Jewish leaders were uneasy before the vision of all Christians once more united in a kind of powerfully organized and closely knit "super-Church" that would proudly bear the marks of pan-Christian exclusiveness and thus imperil, through social pressure, those of other world faiths.

Furthermore, some Jewish leaders asked among themselves: Have the Christians found a cleverly disguised technique slowly to ensnare Jews in the final chamber of Christian ecumenism, in other words, into the pursuit of creedal unity within one Christian family? Proselytism would acquire a different, more acceptable name— ecumenism. This anxiety was enhanced by the fact that the council organ assigned to draft the document and to guide it through the council was called the Secretariat for Promoting Christian Unity.

Yes, the theme of Catholic-Jewish relations might have been too late, but many of us asked, could the topic also be coming too soon? Was Catholic theology prepared for it, and if so, were the bishops prepared for that theology? There had been so little development of the Church's theological and biblical teaching on the mystery of the Jewish people in God's plan of salvation, and on the relationship of Church and Synagogue, and of their shared relationship and common witness to all humanity. Furthermore, catechisms, preaching materials, Bible footnotes, and even liturgical texts were laden with statements that at least implicitly and often unintentionally were fostering the *mépris*. In the words of one of the primary drafters of *Nostra Aetate*, the Jewish question was "the Cinderella on the council agenda." Could Vatican II rouse the Church from her centuries-long sleep and purify her with fresh spirit, thought, and conscience?

Would all the bishops even accept the topic as worthy of a general Church council? Vatican II would reflect a world-wide Church no longer governed mostly by European bishops as the Church had been during Vatican I (1869–70). With one-fifth of the episcopate coming from Latin America, and over one-third from the local churches of Africa, Asia, and Oceania, a schema which concentrated on the guilt and responsibility of Christians with regards to anti-Semitism could easily give the impression that Catholicism, indeed Christianity, was to be simply identified with the old "Western" and "Eastern" churches. Describing their restricted experience as if it were global would be arrogant and so rejected. The local churches of Asia, Africa, and Oceania had not had the same part in this sordid history.

The Secretariat for Promoting Christian Unity itself had an inbuilt problem—the same, in lesser form, with its *Decree on Ecumenism.* In Catholic integrity and with Catholic fidelity, we were trying to establish a sound basis for dialogue with the Jews, without the Church yet having the experience and fruit of such dialogue. If authentic dialogue presumes that we Catholics understand the Jews as they understand themselves to be, and vice versa, then no matter what Vatican II would affirm, its statement would be no more than a basis for *future* dialogue. One of the still persistent naivetes, twenty years later, is to criticize *Nostra Aetate*'s incompleteness or to lament its unanswered questions, as if *Nostra Aetate* had already been a finished product of two decades of dialogue.

Another unanswered question was the political timing of such a document. How much would the political situation in the Middle East, saturated with religious conflict, understandably pressure Catholic leaders of the beleagured minority churches in Arab lands to oppose an explicit treatment of the Jewish question? Any positive development in Catholic-Jewish relations could not be severed from political implications, no matter how theologically and pastorally pure were the conciliar intentions. Although Pope John and Cardinal Bea had been aware of this already in the autumn of 1960, they both, like the rest of us, did not foresee how much counterpressure would be exercised in Middle Eastern church and political circles, through the press and radio and through direct diplomatic channels to the Holy See.

THE WARDI AFFAIR AND OTHER STUMBLING BLOCKS

The first harsh blow came out of the serene blue. On June 12, 1962, Cardinal Bea was at the opening session of the last meeting of the Central Preparatory Committee. Its 102 members already had our schema on the Jews in their hands. Within the next few days Bea was to explain it and plea for its acceptance on the council agenda. Late that same morning of June 12, Monsignor Willebrands, with excited worry, told me in our Secretariat offices that the Secretariat of State had just telephoned. The World Jewish Congress had announced that day its appointment of Dr. Chaim Wardi to serve as "unofficial observer" to the first session of Vatican II. Wardi was the counselor on Christian affairs for the State of Israel's Ministry of Religion. Its minister, Zerah Warhaftig, and the Foreign Minister, Golda Meir, had already publicly endorsed the World Jewish Congress's appointment.

The World Jewish Congress had neither consulted nor informed the Secretariat for Promoting Christian Unity of its act. In the council's strict structure, there was no category of "unofficial observer." We had known from Jewish world leaders of their unpublicized agreement to seek "no representation in any form at the Vatican Council . . . since the council was a Christian theological parley."[6] Moreover, the World Jewish Congress's announcement gave the impression that whereas the Secretariat for Promoting Christian Unity had invited other *religious* communities, albeit only Christian, to have official observers, in the case of the Jews, the Vatican was dealing with a *political* body, the State of Israel, the *"unofficial"* category of observer notwithstanding.

Within two days, Arab diplomats to the Holy See besieged the Secretariat of State with, in Bea's later words, "vociferous protests." Bea supported the immediate consequences of the obvious *faux pas*. He withdrew his schema from the agenda of the convened Central Commission. No presentation, no discussion, no publicity, and no public statement on what quickly was called in both conciliar and Jewish circles, "the Wardi affair." Our fears over the next months were well-warranted: Would the topic itself ever be on the agenda of Vatican II? Secular diplomacy, or the lack of it, seemed to be winning.

The first session itself revealed a council that, however inarticulate may be the consequences, was committed to people as people, whether Catholic or not; was committed to dialogue with others, whether Christian or not. In that very dialogue, the Church would foster its own integrity. Dialogue with other Christians, with the Jews, with all those of other world faiths, indeed with all others, would help the Roman Catholic Church to be Church.

This commitment became more articulate during the second session in the autumn of 1963. The same impetus which asked the question, "Who are these Protestant and Orthodox Christians now living everywhere as neighbors, and what is the Catholic Church's relation with them and their communions?" also asked, "Who are these people of other world faiths, and what is the Catholic Church's relation with them and their faith-communities?"

Within a week after the first session, Bea sent to Pope John a memo which presented a reasoned plea to keep the schema on the council agenda. In a handwritten note, the Pope agreed that the 1960 mandate was still in effect. And the mandate was renewed the next summer by the newly elected Paul VI.[7] The Secrétariat for Promoting Christian Unity thus decided to protect both its beleaguered *De Libertate Religiosa* and its *De Judaeis* by attaching them as concluding chapters to the eagerly awaited schema *On Ecumenism*. The fourth chapter was now entitled, "The Relation of Catholics and Non-Christians, and especially to the Jews." But that chapter gave only polite introductory reference, in two lines, to "conversing and cooperating with non-Christians who nevertheless worship God, or at least with good will, try to follow their conscience in carrying out the moral law situated in human nature."

This brief reference gave leverage to harsh complaints from the bishops, especially those from Asia and Africa: "Two lines for two-thirds of the world!?" The conciliar command: Enlarge the scope of the schema. On the other hand, a solid phalanx of the cardinal patriarchs of ancient Eastern-rite churches in the Middle East—Syrian, Coptic, Melchite, and Armenian—objected to the conciliar propriety of a schema on the Jews. Despite the good intentions of the drafters, they insisted in different ways that Christians in Arab lands have enough difficulties without this gratuitous provocation: ecumenism deals with the Christian family only; if non-Christians are to be treated, do it elsewhere in other schemata, such as "On the Church" or "On the Church in the Modern World."

The Secretariat for Promoting Christian Unity was at first reluctant with the assignment of an enlarged schema. The theme was not within its competency. And above all, the unique character of the Jewish-Christian relation in salvation history might be lost sight of, and the treatment of the specific pastoral problem of anti-Semitism and its roots might not harmonize with the over-all style of the enlarged document and, therefore, would have to be weakened.

Aware of these difficulties, we nevertheless enlisted experts from outside the Secretariat and began the new work—a declaration in five chapters: (1) an introduction on the objective unity of the human family today, a unity of origin, pilgrimage, and ultimate destiny reflected in the universal religious quest for "answers to the profound riddles [*enigmatibus*] of the human condition"; (2) various religions (primitive, Hinduism, Buddhism, etc.; (3) the Islamic religion; (4) the Jewish religion; (5) the condemnation of every kind of discrimination or harrassment because of race, color, condition of life, or religion.

In hindsight, the additional chapters *did* help to gain the support of formerly indifferent bishops, especially from Africa and Asia, and this indirectly helped the Jewish statement, now a chapter within the Declaration. The enlargement protected the Jewish theme, and its opponents, as well as its supporters, knew it. The gem was so embedded into the draft that it could not be removed without crudely disfiguring the whole setting.

In fact, when I consider the pressure that was exerted during the third session, the interim period, and the fourth session either to drop the paragraph on the Jews or to disperse its contents throughout other drafts, the impossible would have remained impossible if there had not been this enlargement.

But more important, *Nostra Aetate* as a whole, primitive and tentative though it may read today, pushed the Church to respond to its own collective consciousness that the majority of the religiously committed people in the world today did not (and do not) live within the Judaeo-Christian tradition. Through the Secretariat's *De Oecumenismo*, *Nostra Aetate*, and *De Libertate Religiosa*, the Church entered the arena of *inclusive* dialogue; none of the outsiders in the post-Vatican II Church and world could be excluded, as the Church exhorts its faithful to "prudently and lovingly, through dialogue and collaboration with the followers of other religions, and in witness to Christian faith and life, acknowledge, preserve, and promote the spiritual and moral goods found among these men and women, as well as the values in their society and culture" (para. 2). The Declaration offered a positive method of dialogue, based upon "what human beings have in common and to what promotes fellowship among them" (para. 1).

Considering pre-Vatican II statements about others, judgments made at a distance under the titles of enemy or tolerated neighbors, this positive methodological approach was an extraordinary step. Not just the single paragraph on the Jews but the all-embracing character of the entire *Nostra Aetate* has since marked its commanding import in Roman Catholic history.

So it was. Twenty years ago, in only fifteen Latin sentences, the impossible became possible, and the possible became act. By their approvals, 2,221 Council Fathers committed the Roman Catholic Church to an irrevocable act, a *heshbon ha-nefesh*, a reconsideration of soul. The act began to shift with integrity 1,900 years of relationships between Catholics and Jews, and to open locks that had been jammed for centuries. That act stirs not pride in our efforts, but humility before God's ways: "The favors of the Lord are not exhausted. . . . His mercies are not spent" (Lam. 3:26).

Twenty years later the short paragraph does not visibly bear the stigmata of the tensions in which it was born. It is still bold and clear, yet in hindsight it is also timid and unware in its assertions:

1. The Church's loving interest in the Jewish people is not due simply to *de facto* religious pluralism, nor is it motivated by guilt. The Church searches into its own mystery. "It remembers the spiritual bonds which tie the people of the New Covenant to the offspring of Abraham." The beginnings of the Church's faith and her election are found already in the patriarchs, Moses, and the prophets. The story of salvation took place within the Jewish people. Jesus, Mary, the apostles, and the early disciples were as much members of that people as the few who were some of the enemies of Jesus. The Jews are God-bearers. The Gentiles are but wild shoots grafted onto the well-cultivated olive tree, which is the Jewish people (cf. Rom. 11:17–24).

2. Judaism is not just another "world religion." The Jews, chosen people, then, today, and always, remain most dear to God. Their election stands, for God neither repents of the gifts He makes nor reneges on the call He issues. No human decision—or Church Council—can break this bond (cf. Rom. 11:28–29).

3. The sins of all men and women, everywhere and at all times, are responsible for Jesus's free acceptance of His passion and death. The cross is a sign of God's all-embracing love, neither a whipping post for any class of people. nor a club to herd people into salvation.

4. Rejected is the continuing "applied culpability" of the Jews; it must never be used in Christian teaching.

Deplored are hatred, persecutions, and manifestations of anti-Semitism directed against the Jews at any time by anyone.

5. Because of the rich patrimony common to Jews and Christians, biblical and theological studies and commended dialogues will, one hopes, foster mutual understanding and esteem. This dialogue is in the wider context of "maintaining good fellowship among the nations" (I Pet. 2:12), of trying to live in peace with all (cf. Rom. 12:18), so that all may truly be sons and daughters of the Father who is in heaven (cf. Matt. 5:45).

THEOLOGICAL QUESTIONS RAISED BUT NOT ANSWERED

In the drafting discussions and in the spoken and written interventions from the Council Fathers, a few major questions arose which the Secretariat decided not to resolve so formally in a conciliar document and to leave to future biblical and theological maturation; also when possible, with the aid of Jewish scholars in the dialogue.

1. The salvation of the Church is "symbolically prefigured [*mystice praesignari*] in the exodus of the chosen people from the land of bondage." From the paschal event, mysteriously prefigured, can one derive principles for the salvation not only of the Jews of "Old Testament" times but also of those Jews who today continue to live within the framework of the Mosaic Law? Furthermore, in this typological theology is the Jewish people not only representative of humanity but also of the Church in a common spiritual destiny?

2. The Church "received the revelation of the Old Testament through the [Israelite] people." But the revelation of the Old Testament continues to be salvific in the Church in the measure that the Church *de facto* con-

tinues to "draw sustenance from the root of that good olive tree" (Rom. 11:17–24). With its subtle Marcionisms, in the measure that the Church *de facto* does *not* draw sustenance, in what ways is the Church less Church? Furthermore, did not the root continue to flourish in the Jewish people during the two millenia of the common era? Is the Church not called to be nourished by that still living Jewish tradition in order to be truly Church?

3. *Nostra Aetate*'s assertion that "the Church is the new People of God" in no way closes discussion on the Jews' being in some way *of* this new People. Nor does the text rule out the theological opinion that a radical schism has divided the People of God on earth into the Church and Israel. Is the schism within the Church or, rather, within Israel?

4. Jesus Christ "reconciled Jew and Gentile, making them both one in Himself" (cf. Eph. 2:14–16). But this reconciliation, which is already realized at its source, is not yet accomplished in history. The theology of history in Romans, chapters 9–11, is a dialectical relationship of Jews and Gentiles, both bound to a common destiny. What is the eschatological destiny, the "fulfillment" of the Jewish people in relation to the nature of their permanent election, and in relation to the incomplete, wounded universality of the Church (Eph. 2) as long as the "proto-schism" is not healed? What is the nature of that *common* messianic and eschatological hope between Jews and Christians—"serve the Lord with one accord" (Zeph. 3:9)—even though there are profoundly different understandings about the forms of the realization of the event?

5. Nothing is to be taught or preached that is "out of harmony with the truth of the Gospel [*cum veritate evangelica non congruat*]." What is the difference between ideological anti-Semitism and the polemic of the evangelists? Do the texts of Matthew and John tend to excuse the disciples and to accuse more and more Jews by excluding

more and more Romans? Who are "the Jews" whom the evangelists accuse, and whom do they represent? For example, what is the typology of "the Jews" in John?

PRESENT QUESTIONS NOT ASKED THEN

Precisely as the fruit of two decades of dialogue which *Nostra Aetate* has solemnly launched, questions which did not arise in the Vatican II ambiance are now on the agenda. But one adds, both in the official Church arena and in Catholic theological circles, there is unevenness in considering the theological and pastoral import of these questions, and there are contrasting Catholic responses. To conclude, then, let me lay some of these questions on the table.

1. Christians in their witness should always avoid proselytism (in the pejorative sense); they should shun all conversionary attitudes and practices which do *not* conform to the ways a free God draws free persons to Himself in response to His calls to serve Him in spirit and in truth (cf. *De Libertate Religiosa*, 2–4). In the case of the Jewish people, also forever the Elect Ones, what is Christian proselytism in practice? And what is "evangelization"—the Church's everlasting proclamation of Jesus Christ, "the Way, the Truth, and the Life (John 14:6–9), in whom all may find the fullness of religious life, and in whom God has reconciled all things to Himself" (cf. 2 Cor. 5:18–19)? Is open dialogue a betrayal of Christian mission? Or is mission a betrayal of dialogue?

2. On the reverse side of the coin, what is the continuing mission of the Synagogue *to* the Church? And what is the *common* mission of the Synagogue and Church, because both are "elected," to humanity, including those of other world faiths?

3. Even though the Council Fathers had already become quite conscious of Europe's Holocaust of European

Jews, Vatican II did not consider how the Holocaust enters into the self-definition of the Jewish people. Nor did the Roman Catholic Church ask how the Holocaust enters into the self-understanding of the Church. Is this event merely another statistic on the indiscriminate listing of "man's inhumanity to man" or but one more in a series of unjust inflictions on the Jews? Not only what *was*, but what *is* this horrendous event in that salvation history in which both Synagogue and Church participate?

4. Vatican II, at least implicitly, regarded the Jews as a peculiar type of denomination or church, at least with the note of their corporate faith-life transcending every nation. The Council did not explicitly consider the Jews as a people who are sustained by a faith that land is the visible expression of the faithful God who wills by covenant the permanence of the Jewish people. Consequently, the Council Fathers did not consider that the post-Holocaust emergence of the State of Israel—the recovery of a promised, found, then long "lost" land—also enters into the self-understanding of most Jews, whether they reside in Israel or not. What is the relationship between the Jewish people and the land, between the land and the State of Israel?

5. Most Council Fathers discussed the urgency of the pastoral ecumenical reflection on the increasing number of "mixed marriages" between Catholics and other Christians. But no mention was made of the radical difference, with immediate pastoral consequences, between the interchurch marriage and one between Jew and Christian.[8]

I conclude with a personal note. A week after the promulgation of *Nostra Aetate*, I was working with the French theologian, René Laurentin, on the history of the text, with commentary, for a popular Paulist Press edition. I now suspect the more seasoned priest detected too much triumphalism in my reaction to the council's text, too much comfort in my naive eyes to the future. He simply asked if I had read the last page of *The Plague* by Camus. No, but I looked it up immediately:

> As Rieux listened to the cries of joy rising from the town, he remembered that such joy could always be imperiled. He knew that those jubilant crowds did not know but could have learned from books: That the plague bacillus never dies or disappears for good; that it can lie dormant for years and years in furniture and linen-chests; that it bides its time in bedrooms, cellars, trunks, and bookshelves; and that perhaps the day would come when, it would rouse up its rats again, and send them forth to die in a happy city.

Indeed, twenty years ago I learned from Camus that with the promulgation of *Nostra Aetate,* Catholics, indeed all Christians, should go ahead, but be more vigilant than ever.

NOTES

1. "The Declaration on Non-Christian Religions," in *Vatican II: An Inter-Faith Appraisal,* ed. John H. Miller, CSC (Notre Dame, Ind.: University of Notre Dame Press, 1966), p. 336.

2. For a detailed history of this Secretariat from its origins in early 1960 to the first session of Vatican II (October 1962), see Thomas F. Stransky, "The Foundation of the Secretariat for Promoting Christian Unity," in *Vatican II Revisited: By Those Who Were There,* ed. Alberic Stacpoole (Minneapolis, Minn.: Winston Press, 1986), pp. 62–87.

3. Capovilla's signed memorandum, March 22, 1966.

4. The unedited account is published in *Service International Documentation Iudeo-Chretienne,* no. 3 (1981); pp. 10–12.

5. Augustin Bea, *The Church and the Jewish People* (New York: Harper and Row, 1966), p. 22.

6. Later, on July 11, 1962, published in *Religious News Service.*

7. Bea's memorandum and John XXIII's response in the official *Acta Synodalia* (Vatican City: Vatican Polyglot Press,

1970), II, p. 485. For Paul VI's confirmation, in audience with Bea, see Bea, op. cit., 159.

8. Much of the above is repeated or elaborated in my "Focusing on Jewish-Catholic Relations" in *Origins,* June 20, 1985; "The Catholic-Jewish Dialogue: Twenty Years after *Nostra Aetate*" in *America,* February 8, 1986; "Reflections on *Nostra Aetate*" in *The Month,* May 1986.

5. *Nostra Aetate*:
A Typology of Theological Tendencies

WENDELL S. DIETRICH

> Let me say now, quite sharply, that there are signifi-
> cant advantages for Jews and Judaism in attaining in
> Christian theological eyes the status of just one more
> non-Christian religion. Attaining that status at least
> eases off the pressure of the Christian obsession with
> Judaism and with the origins of Christianity out of first
> century Judaism. Perhaps Jews should savor their lib-
> eration in this connection.

Thomas Stransky's paper "Holy Diplomacy: Making the
Impossible Possible" reminds us of the glory and misery
of Christian theology. In describing and analyzing the
history and content of *Nostra Aetate,* Stransky documents
what disciplined theological inquiry in a community like
the Roman Catholic Church can accomplish.[1] Thus, a
reminder of the glory of Christian theology. Stransky
also informs us about how difficult it is for theological
activity to be deployed accurately to produce religious
clarity and rationality in the midst of clashes of power
politics and social antagonisms and in the face of misunderstandings and hostilities among religious communities. Thus, a reminder of theology's misery.

In my own judgment as a historian of modern Christian thought and of modern Judaic thought, *Nostra Aetate*

70

registers a major accomplishment for Christian theology and a decisive and irreversible shift in Roman Catholic teaching about Jews and Judaism. That anything at all on this topic was forthcoming at the Second Vatican Council is noteworthy. On the other hand, the teaching of paragraph 4 of *Nostra Aetate* is in many respects quite elementary and undeveloped. Moreover, any reader of Father John Oesterreicher's extensive commentary on the "Declaration" in the standard Herder and Herder *Commentary on the Documents of Vatican II*[2] will have further reinforced the sense Stransky conveys: the sense of how precarious the situation was throughout the debates at the council and how close the whole enterprise came to being swept away in the currents and countercurrents of political and religious confusion and hostility.

Beyond these broad considerations, Thomas Stransky's paper reminds us that the construction of *Nostra Aetate* and its paragraph 4 involved unique problems quite different from Vatican II's work on other topics. As Stransky puts it, in decisive respects the declaration came too late, and yet, it also came too soon.

To say that it came too late is to acknowledge that the Holocaust had already occurred. Modern man in Western civilization had already conceived and executed with unprecedented technical efficiency the planned destruction of six million Jews. No one can, admittedly, estimate with entire precision the extent to which the traditional Christian "teaching of contempt" for the Jews made possible and contributed to the ethos in which the Holocaust occurred. But without doubt that "teaching of contempt" was a contributing factor and *Nostra Aetate*'s about-face came too late to head off the Holocaust.

But, in another respect, as Stransky points out, the teaching of *Nostra Aetate* came too soon. In no other area in which Vatican II attempted to make a major statement was the state of theological preparation so primitive. For example, "The Constitution on the Sacred Liturgy" brought to fruition a half century of historical and theological inquiry. In the case of "The Dogmatic Constitution on the Church" and "The Dogmatic Constitution on Divine Revelation," a corps of theologians had been quietly working away on these topics for a couple of decades—sometimes in the face of official suspicion and hostility. "The Pastoral Constitution on the Church in the Modern World"—in many ways Vatican II's greatest achievement—made use of two generations of path-breaking theoretical work. And the American John Courtney Murray and the French theologians of the freedom of the act of faith were surely ready to lay out a rationale for religious liberty.

Nothing like that obtained in the case of *Nostra Aetate* and its paragraph 4 on the Jews and Judaism. There had been up to the time of Vatican II a conspicuous lack of disciplined reflection on what I choose to call a "Christian theology of Judaism." And that is what Stransky quite correctly means by saying the "Declaration" came too soon.

THEOLOGICAL TENDENCIES AND IMPULSES

Since it is clear that the state of theological investigation of the topics of *Nostra Aetate* was by no means mature at the time of Vatican II, what can we say about the diverse theological tendencies and impulses that played into the final formulation of *Nostra Aetate*? I propose now to refer once again to Stransky's account of the history of the document's evolution but also to attempt somewhat independently to lay out a typology of theological tendencies. If that typology is properly constructed, it will also help us to understand and appraise the very considerable development beyond *Nostra Aetate*, 4, to be found in the 1975 "Guidelines and Suggestions for Jewish-Christian Relations,"[3] issued by the Committee for Religious Relations with the Jews, and even to understand and appraise more accurately the much controverted June 1985 document "Notes on the Correct Way to Present Jews and Judaism in Preaching and Cathechesis in the Roman Catholic Church."[4]

In my typology of theological tendencies operative in the formulation of *Nostra Aetate*, I propose four types: (1) a simple affirmative declaration about the Jews in acknowledgment of the errors of the traditional teaching of contempt for the Jews; (2) a social ethical impulse grounded in the necessity for mutual respect among various social groups that are in increasingly close interaction in modern global society; (3) a new positive attitude toward non-Christian religions accompanied by a general theory of non-Christian religions; and, (4) a Christian theology of Judaism based on a fresh reading of the Pauline teaching about the Jews in Romans 9–11.

THE TEACHING OF CONTEMPT

The history of the evolution of *Nostra Aetate*, 4, clearly demonstrates that a simple affirmative declaration revising the teaching of contempt was what Pope John XXIII and Cardinal Bea initially had in mind. They conceived of a "Declaration on the Jews" not set in any broader Christian theological or social ethical context. Such a "Declaration" would be responsive to the agenda set by Jewish spokesmen like Jules Isaac of France.

It is useful even now to review Isaac's classic specification of the elements of the traditional "teaching of contempt" for the Jews. Isaac[5] singled out, first, teaching about the "dispersion of the Jews as a providential punishment for the crucifixion"; second, traditional and even modern scholarly teaching about the "degenerate state of Judaism at the time of Jesus"; and, third, specific allegations about the Jews as a "deicide people." *Nostra Aetate*, 4, and indeed also the subsequent 1975 "Guidelines" and the 1985 "Notes" all repudiate the traditional teaching of contempt.

MUTUAL RESPECT: A SOCIAL-ETHICAL
IMPULSE

But apparently that simple affirmative statement was
always a declaration in search of a deeper context. The
history of the debate at Vatican II recounted by Stransky
indicates several alternative contexts. This leads to my
second type of theological tendency.

In laying out this second type I leap over the narrative
chronicle of the stages of *Nostra Aetate*'s formulation and
look directly at the completed text. My second type is a
social-ethical impulse grounded in the necessity for
mutual respect among various social groups that are in
increasingly close interaction in modern global society. I
should be inclined to give this impulse more of an independent status than Stransky does in his paper.

Consider the language of the opening paragraph of
the document:

> In our times, when every day men are being drawn closer
> together and the ties between various peoples are being
> multiplied, the Church is giving deeper study to her rela-
> tionship with non-Christian religions. In her task of foster-
> ing unity and love among men, and even among nations,
> she gives primary consideration in this document to what
> human beings have in common and to what promotes fel-
> lowship among them.

This line of argumentation connects *Nostra Aetate* to Vatican II's "Constitution on the Church in the Modern
World" and to Pope John XXIII's great encyclicals on
world peace and social justice, *Pacem in Terris* and *Mater et
Magistra*. It also fits in with the "Declaration on Religious
Liberty" and with those truths that John Courtney Murray insisted the whole Catholic world must learn from the
American political and social experience: truths about
limited government, the protection of religious liberty by
constitutional guarantees, and the benefits of religious
pluralism.

A THEORY OF NON-CHRISTIAN RELIGIONS

The simple affirmative declaration reversing the teaching of contempt was apparently a declaration in search of a context, and the context it finally found was in a "Declaration on Non-Christian Religions." It is in fact the case that in the final order of presentation, paragraph 4 on the Jews and Judaism has to wait patiently in line behind positive theological appraisals of Hinduism, of Buddhism, and of Islam. But what can we say in detail about the general theory of non-Christian religions that informs these positive appraisals and thus shapes the document as a whole (my third type of impulse behind *Nostra Aetate*)? To be absolutely faithful to the text, I should have to acknowledge that it is not entirely clear what that general theory of non-Christian religions is. Each of the great religious traditions—Hinduism, Buddhism, Islam, and by implication Judaism—apparently contains some religious truth which can be appropriately acknowledged by Christians. But do we have here, as some of the commentators at first thought, simply a replay of the classic *Logos* doctrine of the second century Christian apologists, according to which the partial and distorted truths of non-Christian religions find fulfillment and completion in Christianity? Perhaps. But I offer the hypothesis that something more radical is at work here.

Clearly within the general theological resources available to the Bishops and their experts at Vatican II was a striking revision of the doctrine of grace and a reappraisal of the salvific, in the strongest sense, character and function of non-Christian religions. I refer to the development of the Catholic doctrine of grace worked out by the German Catholic theologian Karl Rahner and his school. Although this theory of grace is not specifically invoked by *Nostra Aetate,* the declaration is compatible with Rahner's doctrine of grace and the salvific character and function of non-Christian religions. I venture to suggest further that it is through the prism of Rahner's doctrine that many Catholic theologians have subsequently read the teaching of *Nostra Aetate*.

According to those views of Rahner and his school, the positive impact on humanity of the presence of God in Christ is so irreversible and pervasive that the salvific grace of God, which is indeed the grace of Christ, can be discerned by the Christian in the secular heroes and champions of social justice of the modern world. Moreover, this same grace can also be seen to be operative in the non-Christian religions.

To the outsider, this may look like yet one more version of traditional theological imperialism. Internal to the structure of Catholic faith and life, Rahner's teaching has effected a reversal of a traditional Catholic theological thesis. Traditionally, the Church is the ordinary means of salvation and on the margins one may talk about extraordinary means of salvation. In the perspective of the new doctrine of grace, the Church, in terms of empirically discerned operation and even intrinsically, is the extraordinary means of salvation. The Church is a diaspora Church, a dispersed minority in a global world culture. The ordinary means through which men receive salvation are situations outside the Church including, among other settings, the non-Christian religions.

I should myself be inclined to argue that, whatever actual historical impact Rahner's doctrine had on the formulation of *Nostra Aetate,* in any case such a doctrine would be the best possible base for establishing poise and confidence in a new style of Christian encounter with non-Christian religions.

PAULINE TEACHING: ROMANS 9–11

Finally, a fourth theological tendency, a Christian theology of Judaism based on a fresh reading of the Pauline teaching about the Jews in Romans, chapters 9–11, very likely informed Thomas Stransky's participation in the composition of the document and deeply informs his paper printed in this book.

The history of the evolution of *Nostra Aetate* shows that the positive declaration on Jews and Judaism did not initially find lodging in a *Declaration on Non-Christian Religions*. Indeed, that positive declaration on Jews and Judaism at first found shelter in the *Decree on Ecumenism,* a decree about the restoration of the unity and wholeness of the Christian religious community. *Nostra Aetate,* 4, still shows the marks of that. The opening words of paragraph 4 are quite out of synchronization with previous statements about Hinduism, Buddhism, and Islam. Astonishingly enough, paragraph 4 begins, "As this sacred Synod searches into the mystery of the Church, it recalls the spiritual bond linking the people of the New Covenant with Abraham's stock." Great care is lavished on demonstrating the roots of the Christ and the Christian Church in the people of Israel. A vision of the future is projected which anticipates a unified total humanity in which believers in Christ and Jews are reconciled. The great asset of such teaching, explicitly warranted by Romans 9–11, is that it permits an unequivocal statement that God's covenant with the Jewish people has never been revoked. This secures a decisive repudiation of the traditional Christian teaching about the supersession of the Jewish people by the Church as the elect people of God.

It is as a further development of the Pauline vision that I read some of the most important new European theological work on the Christian theology of Judaism, such as Clemens Thoma's *A Christian Theology of Judaism*[6] and Franz Mussner's *Tractate on the Jews: The Significance of Judaism for Christian Faith*[7]. In Mussner's work, we even find the possibility that a Pauline vision of final reconciliation between Jews and Christians and a declaration

about the ultimate salvation of the Jews need not necessarily imply an expectation of the final conversion of the
Jews, as if their salvation were contingent on their recognition of Jesus as Messiah.

However, I want to state as bluntly as possible that,
although such a Pauline theology of Judaism secures the
irrevocable character of God's covenant with the people
Israel, such a theology is very much an internal Christian
theological vision. That accounts in part for the fact that
in *Nostra Aetate* there is absolutely no recognition of the
actual richness, diversity, and vitality of Jewish religious
life after the first century. For any such recognition one
had to wait for the first tentative initiatives of the 1975
"Guidelines." In the 1975 "Guidelines," the Jewish liturgical tradition is recognized, as is the classic Judaic witness to the transcendence and unicity of God.

THE PRESENT STATE OF THE QUESTION

As Thomas Stransky points out, there are still on the
agenda items of the same order as the items which
prompted the simple positive declaration about Jews and
Judaism, the reversal of the teaching of contempt. By
way of illustration, consider the negative reaction in June
1985 by some spokesmen for Jewish agencies to the new
"Notes on the Correct Way to Present Jews and Judaism
in Preaching and Cathechesis in the Roman Catholic
Church." Why, such Jewish spokesmen inquired with
striking directness, don't Catholics acknowledge officially the significance of the Holocaust for Christians as well
as for Jews? Why don't Catholics have more to say about
the State of Israel than merely that: "Christians are invited to understand this [Jewish] religious attachment [to
the memory of the land of their forefathers] which finds
its roots in biblical tradition, without [Catholic Chris-
tians], however, making their own any particular reli-

gious interpretation of this relationship" and, "The existence of the State of Israel and its political options should be envisaged not in a perspective which is in itself religious, but in their reference to the common principles of international law"? A contemporary Jules Isaac might well be pressing these questions. But, on the other hand, I should want to insist that their resolution is a matter of great complexity.

Especially on the American scene, I believe, continuing attention is properly given to a social-ethical impulse grounded in the necessity for mutual respect among various social groups that are in increasingly close interaction in modern global society. It may well be the particular responsibility of the American Catholic Bishops and their theological experts to make sure that, in the international Church of the 1980s as well as the 1960s, the significance of American religious pluralism is not slighted.

Finally, what about the most strictly theological impulses: the placing of Judaism as a non-Christian religion in the context of a general theory of the salvific character and function of non-Christian religion and a Pauline Christian theology of Judaism?

I have already conceded that a theory of the salvific function of non-Christian religions like Rahner's may strike the outsider as another piece of Christian theological imperialism. But let me now say, quite sharply, that there are significant advantages for Jews and Judaism in attaining in Christian theological eyes the status of just one more non-Christian religion. Attaining that status at least eases off the pressure of the Christian obsession with Judaism and with the origins of Christianity out of first-century Judaism. Perhaps Jews should savor their liberation in this connection.

A Christian theology of Judaism based on Romans 9–11 obviously is well-warranted in Christian theological sources. Such a theology secures the irrevocability of

God's covenant with the people of Israel. Such a theology of Judaism is, in effect, all that came to explicit expression in *Nostra Aetate*. That is one of the reasons I called *Nostra Aetate*'s theology quite elementary and primitive. In my judgment, this Pauline theology can be and is being further developed. I am not disposed to recommend against such development, but I suggest that there are other equally fruitful points of departure for a Christian theology of Judaism that could profitably be explored and assessed.

The issues, as I have framed them, I hope are clear. As Christians and Jews, we have now to continue the discussions begun twenty years ago.

NOTES

1. In preparing this paper, I made use of these texts of *Nostra Aetate*: "Declaration on the Relationship of the Church to Non-Christian Religions," in Walter M. Abbott, S.J., ed., *The Documents of Vatican II* (New York: Guild Press, America Press, Association Press, 1966), pp. 660–668, and "Les Relations de l'Eglise avec les religions non chretiennes: Declaration 'Nostra aetate'," Texte latin et traduction francaise (Paris: Les Editions du Cerf, 1966). In addition, I was guided by Henry Siegman, "A Decade of Catholic-Jewish Relations: A Reassessment," in *Journal of Ecumenical Studies* 15 (1978): pp. 243–260, and Michael Wyschogrod, "A New State in Jewish-Christian Dialogue," in *Judaism* 31 (1982): pp. 356–365.

2. John M. Oesterreicher, "Declaration on the Relationship of the Church to Non-Christian Religions: Introduction and Commentary," in Herbert Vorgrimler, ed., *Commentary on the Documents of Vatican II*, vol. III (New York: Herder and Herder, 1967), pp. 1–136.

3. "Guidelines on Religious Relations with the Jews (N. 4)," Committee for Religious Relations with the Jews, December 1, 1974, in Austin Flannery, ed., *Vatican Council II: The Conciliar and Post-Conciliar Documents* (Collegeville, Minn.: Liturgical Press, 1975), pp. 743–749.

4. "Notes on the Correct Way to Present Jews and Judaism in Preaching and Cathechesis in the Roman Catholic Church," Commission for Religious Relations with the Jews, June 24, 1985, in *Origins* 15:4 (July 4, 1985): pp. 102–107.

5. Jules Isaac, *The Teaching of Contempt: Christian Roots of Anti-Semitism* (New York: Holt, Rinehart, and Winston, 1964).

6. Clemens Thoma, *A Christian Theology of Judaism* (Mahwah, N.J.: Paulist Press, 1980).

7. Franz Mussner, *Tractate on the Jews: The Significance of Judaism for Christian Faith* (Philadelphia: Fortress Press, 1984).

6. A Very Small Lever
Can Move the Entire World

DANIEL F. POLISH

> In *The Caine Mutiny* Herman Wouk uses the image of a
> massive door turning on a tiny ball bearing. The mo-
> ment of *Nostra Aetate* twenty years ago was like that ball
> bearing. A whole movement, a whole world turned on
> it. And the world never again will be the same.

Since Vatican II, the Church as a whole has been going
through a radical transformation: in the way that it views
the world in general, in the way that it defines its place in
the world, and in its own structure. In fact, we have seen
in these twenty years a religious institution reformulat-
ing itself in scope and in speed, unprecedented in the
history of human religiousness. Twenty years is a very
brief time, *sub species Aeternitatus,* and in the slow work-
ings of religious institutions. And yet, in that brief time,
we have lived through a major transformation.

It is important for Jews to remember that the changes
that are articulated in *Nostra Aetate* represent only one
part of the work of the council. The entirety of Vatican
II, contrary to our perception, is not devoted to the
question of the Jews. The council was not called to
address itself to who we are or who we are not. We would

do well to come to understand the changes in the
Church's attitude toward the Jews in the context of that
whole transvaluation.

BEFORE VATICAN II

All of us are familiar with the conditions that existed
before Vatican II: the pull of the Marcionistic tendencies, and that litany well known to us all—the crusades,
the Inquisition expulsions, and so forth. There were less
dramatic expressions as well. For me the attitude of the
Catholic Church toward the Jewish people was epito-
mized in Theodor Herzl's audience with Pope Pius X in
1904. Herzl, the father of political Zionism, went to the
Pope to ask for his assistance in creating the *Altneuland,*
the "old-new land" in what is today *Medinat Yisrael,* the
State of Israel. The Pope's response is suggestive. He
said:

> We cannot favor this movement. The Jews did not recog-
> nize Jesus Our Lord, and therefore we cannot recognize the
> Jewish people. If you come to Palestine and settle your
> people there, we will be ready with priests and churches to
> baptize all of you.[1]

There is a footnote to this incident. This statement by
Pope Pius X was echoed, I believe, even by Angelo Car-
dinal Roncalli, when he was the Papal Nuncio in Istanbul.
This man, who was to become the great and good Pope
John XIII, did make baptismal certificates available to
Jews, for the best of reasons—to save them from Nazi
persecution.

But, in a letter to Cardinal Luigi Maglione, the Vatican
Secretary of State, in 1943, he stressed his reservations
about one part of what he was doing. He said, "It does not
seem in good taste that this work of saving Jewish lives,"
(and here his use of words, I think, is interesting) "should

help in the realization of their messianic dream." And, he goes on, "Perhaps this is just a personal scruple of mine. In any case, it is certain that the reconstruction of the reign of Judah and Israel is nothing but a utopia."

And relatedly, when his successor, Pope Paul VI, visited Israel (about which more will be said later), his relation to Israel and to the Jewish people was at best ambivalent. This occurred between the second and the third sessions of the Council—before the ratification of *Nostra Aetate*. He could only talk about the past significance of the Jewish people. He could note what that people, when it was alive, as it were, did in the Land. He would bring himself neither to speak of the current historical reality nor of the meaning of the survival of the people and their return to the Land. Those ideas would be enabled only by the document which was to be promulgated two years after his visit.

So much for what the Catholic-Jewish dialogue was like on a more global level before *Nostra Aetate*. On a more personal level, all of us have memories of what the relations between Jews and Catholics were like—the pain of Catholic friends, who might be invited to celebrate in the life-cycle experience of a Jew in a synagogue, who had to get specific dispensation to attend the services, and on getting such dispensation were warned, "but you may not participate in the service." Jews of a generation only one older than mine, who came from Europe, still hold vivid memories of the fear that came every year with the arrival of Holy Week. Even many American Jews harbor memories of their consistent fear of being beaten by students coming out of parochial school—the fear of even walking in front of a Catholic church, let alone venturing inside. All of that is part of the history of Jewish-Catholic relations before *Nostra Aetate*. All of this is testimony to the hostility that existed on so many levels between Jews and Catholics, as well as between the Jewish religious tradition and the Catholic religious tradition.

Now we celebrate a very different world. In fact, our world is so transformed from that world that we have almost lost sight of the magnitude of the transformation. We take for granted the amicable relations that exist, the openness of dialogue and freedom of communication. It is hard for us to summon up what took place twenty years ago. And yet it is clear that something profound happened at that council.

I need not rehearse what *Nostra Aetate* stated. Instead I would like to look at two major points—and some minor ones—about the document.

DELIBERATION AND POLITICS

The first point on which I would like to dwell at some length is that the document did not spring like Athena from the brow of the Council Fathers. There was a complex process of deliberation and even political maneuvering involved in *Nostra Aetate*'s creation. And, significantly, the Jewish community played an important role in that complex of deliberation and of maneuvering, and in shaping the statement that spoke about Jews and Jewish life.[2]

When the council was convened in October 1962, Jews were not included among the number of official observers, or even of officially invited guests. Nonetheless, a process of regular consultation had emerged even before the beginning of the council itself. There is an important prehistory. As Thomas Stransky's paper makes clear, Jules Isaac visited the Pope in June of 1960 and talked to him about the idea of the contempt. Three months after that, the Pope ordered the Secretariat for the Promotion of Christian Unity to draft a declaration on the Jewish question.

The World Jewish Congress and the International B'nai B'rith submitted to the Secretariat a joint memorandum on the subject of anti-Semitism. The American Jewish Committee submitted a number of papers on such issues as the image of the Jew in Catholic teaching and anti-Jewish elements in Catholic liturgy.

Before the formal convocation of the council, a spokesman came on the scene who would play an incalculable role in articulating Jewish concerns to the framers of *Nostra Aetate*. Rabbi Abraham Joshua Heschel was a prominent scholar and a figure of commanding authority. At several crucial junctures in the deliberations, Heschel was to visit Rome and speak in behalf of the cause of the Jewish people. His first visit was in November 1961. He would return to Rome at the beginning of the third session, when he had a private audience with the Pope on the opening day of the session. His visit, on that occasion, was at the request of the American delegation. He is credited with changing the thinking of many of the Council Fathers and effecting the final outcome of the decision.

Throughout the council the Jewish community followed the deliberations closely and, through various means, communicated its concerns to the Council Fathers. In a remarkable and unprecedented way, the Jewish community managed to have some involvement in shaping an official document of the Catholic Church. This participation was symbolized by the greeting and message sent by Dr. Elio Toaff, the Chief Rabbi of Rome, the first such greeting ever conveyed by a Jewish leader to a Church council.

Representatives of the Jewish community found themselves engaged in specific and significant issues throughout the council. The question of where any statement on the Jews ought properly be lodged emerged at the beginning of the second session. There was disagreement within the council itself, and of course, as you can expect, there was disagreement within the Jewish community. There were those who thought that any statement on the

Jews should be placed in the schema on ecumenism, because it is there that certain theological issues would be hammered out. That seemed a desirable location, for the question of the Jews would be addressed in a theological context. On the other hand, there were those who argued against putting it in the schema on ecumenism, in the context of Church unity, since that might be perceived as having negative theological implications. To talk about the Jews in the context of unity among people of various groups might reduce that statement to another ploy in the two-millennia-old battle for the Jewish soul, to encumber it with conversionary overtones.

Some then favored placing a statement on the Jews in a schema on world problems. But many in the Jewish community argued against defining the Jews as a problem and felt that the relationship of the Church and the Jews was of a different magnitude than other "world problems." They noted that a special relationship exists between Judaism and Christianity and felt that that relationship ought properly be embodied in any statement. The involvement of Jewish agencies increased greatly during the third session when it appeared that no statement, or a very weak one, would be forthcoming. Representatives of various Jewish groups in America spoke to Catholic audiences about their concerns and urged that Jewish leaders arrange to meet with their local bishops to explain the concern of the Jewish community and solicit the support of the bishops.

At this time Dr. Joseph Lichten of the Anti-Defamation League of B'nai B'rith spent an increasing amount of time in Rome. It was Lichten who was responsible for each delegate's receiving a copy of a study by two sociologists, Charles Clock and Rodney Stark, about Christian beliefs and anti-Semitism. The findings of that study were both revealing and disturbing.

The study indicated that 61 percent of Catholics in America felt that Jews are the group most responsible for the crucifixion of Jesus. Forty-six percent of Catholics agreed with, or were uncertain, about the statement that, "Jews can *never* be forgiven for what they did to Jesus, until they accept Him as their true savior."

Lichten, in Rome, summarized the findings as follows:

> Perhaps as many as five million American Catholics, out of a total of forty-four, or almost forty-five million, see the Jews as principally responsible for the death of Jesus, and they are led thereby to a negative assessment of the contemporary Jew. The fact that those who believe and feel this way tend to go to church more frequently underscores the need for the Catholic Church to intensify its efforts if it hopes to win all Catholics to the principles of brotherhood which it espouses.

Jewish involvement in the council was not without its negative consequences. At the conclusion of the first session, a number of tracts were circulated to the Council Fathers which were crudely anti-Semitic in character.

The fact is that the tracts were aimed less at the Jews than at liberals in the council. The conservative authors of the texts were less concerned with Jews and Judaism than in defaming their ideological opponents. Thus they chose to depict liberals as a "Jewish fifth column inside the Church." Jews were caught in the familiar position of being the interstitial victim in someone else's quarrel.

Nonetheless, the distribution of these documents was a source of apprehension for the Jewish community, arousing fear about the possible direction the council might go. For the Council Fathers, the release of those tracts seems to have had a paradoxical effect. For many it was the first real exposure to sentiments of this nature. As such, they served to substantiate the concerns, expressed by Jewish spokesmen, about the role of Church teaching in fostering contempt and hatred of the Jews.

The unprecedented indirect "participation" of the Jewish community in the deliberations of the council no doubt made an impact on the shape of the document that was eventually adopted. Most certainly it gave the Council Fathers a sense of the seriousness with which their work was being followed in the Jewish community.

JEWISH RESPONSE: ENTHUSIASTIC OR SKEPTICAL

This seriousness is reflected in statements of various Jewish leaders of the period. They express a wide divergence of opinions about the importance of any statement on the Jews and its implications for Jewish life.

As the second session began, Rabbi Maurice Eisendrath, President of the Union of American Hebrew Congregations, the congregational body of the Reform movement, spoke in a mood of great optimism about what was taking place in Rome. Eisendrath reflects the enthusiasm that some in the Jewish community felt for the statement as it was taking shape, going so far as to suggest the need for some kind of reciprocal gesture:

> We Jews have long clamored for this indispensable change in official Catholic dissemination of fact and interpretation. But what about our Jewish attitudes toward Christendom, toward Jesus especially? Are we to remain adamant, orthodox, in our refusal to examine our statements, our own facts, our own interpretations on the significance of the life of Jesus the Jew? Have we examined our own books, official and otherwise, to reappraise our oftimes jaundiced view of him in whose name Christianity was established? How long shall we continue pompously to aver that the chief contribution of Jesus was simply a rehash of all that had been said before by his Jewish ancestors? How long before we can admit that his influence was a beneficial one, not only to the pagans, but to the Jews of his time as well, and that only those who later took his name in vain profaned his teaching?

On the other hand, as the second session proceeded, Jews noticed that the document contained significant deficiencies—most glaringly that the Church took too little responsibility for anti-Semitism and did not talk about its own contribution to anti-Semitism. Some took issue with the tone of the document. It seemed that the Church was absolving the Jews for crimes of which they considered themselves never to have been guilty. That dimension of Jewish thinking was expressed most vehemently from the Orthodox sector of the community.

Norman Lamm, currently the President of Yeshiva University, at that time already an influential thinker in the Orthodox community, wrote in the official publication of the Union of Orthodox Jewish Congregations of America, the Orthodox counterpoint to Eisendrath's organization. If Eisendrath is overly irenic on one side, Lamm, it seems, is somewhat shrill on the other. Lamm writes:

> As Jews we object to being absolved of the guilt of killing their God. To be absolved implies that one is guilty, but that nevertheless he is being forgiven. But we Jews never were guilty, and we do not therefore beg forgiveness. To our mind the question is not who will absolve the Jews. The question is, who will absolve the Church for its guilt in inspiring and sponsoring crusades and inquisitions, blood libels and pogroms? The Church has expressed to the Jewish people neither apology nor confessions nor regrets.

At various points in the deliberations of the council, members of the Jewish community expressed fear that no statement would be adopted; at other points that a statement would be issued that was too weak to have any meaning or any potential for impact on Catholic thought. At certain moments, some Jews feared that a statement would be issued that was actually hostile and inimical to Jewish welfare. When it became clear that the statement would assume roughly the form of the one that

was ultimately adopted, a new concern was expressed—
the fear that the real intent of any statement on the Jews
was missionary in character.

Of the various reactions to the work in progress, the
one with perhaps the most enduring consequences was
that of Rabbi Joseph Soloveitchik, preeminent idealogue
of the modern Orthodox branch of Judaism in America.
During the third session Rabbi Soloveitchik published an
article in which he called for a prohibition on discussing
theology with non-Jews. The hidden intent of such conversations, he argued, is evangelistic, and the ultimate
consequence may be apostasy. Soloveitchik noted that
Jews have much to talk with Christians about: history;
social issues; literature. But theological discussions are
unproductive and even potentially destructive. It is clear
in retrospect that this opinion, still the definitive stance
within the Orthodox community, was a direct response
to the proceedings of the Vatican Council.

Jewish perception of the potential outcome of the
council was influenced by two actions of Pope Paul VI in
the midst of the council. Between the second and third
sessions, the Pope visited Israel. It is clear that the Pope
resonated to the spiritual dimension of his "pilgrimage."
Jews watched for its political implications. Throughout
that trip, the Pope never mentioned the name Israel.
Moreover he insisted on addressing Israel's then President Zalman Shazar solely as "your Excellency," without
reference to his elected position. This very circumspect
behavior produced a sense of unease in Jewish interpre-
ters of the events.

That sense of foreboding was exacerbated by the
Pope's Lenten homily in 1965, just before the beginning
of the fourth session. In that homily, he took recourse to
familiar deicide imagery. It was imagery of the precise
nature that the Jewish community had hoped the council
would eliminate. Many Jews interpreted the Pope's use
of the old idiom as an indication of the thinking of the

council as a whole. Fortunately, it was not predictive of the ultimate direction the document would take, but the immediate result was to arouse apprehension and even anger among many Jews.

As the fourth session began, there was fear in the Jewish community that a constructive statement would never emerge. Jews expressed coolness to the proceedings and to the statement that was then under consideration. The most salient expression of that coolness was enacted around the Pope's visit to the United States which occurred during this time. Though many Jews were invited to meet the Pope or attend various gatherings with him, almost none accepted these invitations. This was symbolic of Jewish unhappiness with the Pope's own words and deeds, but no less representative of a more generalized Jewish mood before the opening of the fourth session. The Pope was to some extent the cause of, and in this instance the lightning rod for, a pervasive sense of skepticism within the Jewish community about the outcome of the Council's deliberations.

NOSTRA AETATE AND GEOPOLITICS

In assessing the influences that were at work in shaping *Nostra Aetate,* it is possible that the most significant factor is one that seems incongruous in the context of theological deliberations: geopolitics, specifically the geopolitics of the Middle East.

Just as the Jewish community had a keen interest on the deliberations that would yield a new church attitude toward the Jews, a no-less intense interest was evident from the Arab world.

I have noted the activities of the Jewish community surrounding the writing of *Nostra Aetate.* It is remarkable and suggestive that the Arab world was reciprocally engaged in trying to shape the document to make it conform to its own purposes.

While the Jewish community, naturally enough, had no voice within the council, Arab concerns were articulated by representatives of Arab Christian communities and leaders of Eastern communions. While the Jewish world had no accredited observers at the deliberations, representatives of Arab states which had diplomatic relations with the Vatican were present as official guests and afforded themselves of the opportunity to express themselves forcefully.

After the first session, Gustave Weigel, a Jesuit who served on Cardinal Bea's Secretariat, told a meeting of the National Jewish Community Relations Advisory Council that the reason no statement on the Jews emerged from that first session was because of the pressure of the Arab world. Weigel left the impression that the Arabs had succeeded in having the statement withdrawn. The Secretariat for Promoting Christian Unity had to respond to the anxiety that Weigel's statement aroused. Interestingly, while disagreeing with Weigel, it couched the issues in terms of the same political situation. It denied that the withdrawl was effected in response to Arab pressure, and insisted that it was caused by the Wardi incident described in Thomas Stransky's paper. The Secretariat argued that the Wardi affair caused such embarrassment to the council that the statement had to be withdrawn for its own welfare.

The same political overtones emerged a little bit later, after the second session began. On October 16, the statement in its then current form was leaked to the *New York Times*. The question, as always, was who was responsible for such leaks. The supposition was that it was leaked by its supporters, who hoped that its appearance in public would arouse such positive response that it would generate pressure on the Council Fathers to adopt this statement.

At any rate, when the statement was leaked, Cardinal Bea had to make a response to it, and his choice of what to focus on is interesting. Cardinal Bea said that the document "is religious in intent and spiritual in purpose, and cannot be called pro-Zionist, since those questions (questions of Zionism) are political questions entirely outside the scope of the statement." It is interesting to note the way that the issue came to be addressed in terms of whether it was pro-Zionist or not pro-Zionist.

The crucial question, in this regard, is why the Arab world had any interest at all in a statement by the Catholic Church about the Jews. This interest cannot be attributed to some kind of malevolence or mindless Jew-hatred among enemies of the State of Israel. On the contrary, this jockeying between the Jewish world and the Arab world is quite significant. Indeed, the involvement of the Arab world was motivated by the exact obverse of the political dimension of the concerns that impelled the Jewish community.

Whether consciously articulated, or intuited at some unconscious level, Jews and Arabs had both perceived a central reality in the Church's theology of the Jews: the relationship of the deicide charge to the Jewish condition of exile. Implicit in Church dogma until *Nostra Aetate* was the belief that the rejecton of Jesus by the Jews was responsible for their dispersion. Exile was a visible punishment for deicide.

Jews and Arabs alike recognized—again, on either a conscious or preconscious level—that for the Church to absolve the Jews of the charge of deicide would, by implication, remove the major *theological* justification for denying them the right to a homeland. In recognizing, alike, the implications of this change in theological stance, Arabs and Jews came to diametrically opposite conclusions about their proper course of action. The Arab world operated on the assumption of the necessity of upholding the charge of deicide to preserve a Catholic rationale for opposing a Jewish homeland. The energy for Jewish activity in the opposite direction must have derived from the sense that the elimination of the deicide charge would draw in its wake, among other consequences, the elimination of the necessity for the Church to oppose the legitimacy of Jewish political aspirations. Thus Arab involvement in the deliberations of the Vatican Council, as well as some measure of Jewish concern, was motivated by considerations that can be characterized as "political." This impingement of political considerations on theological deliberation is not without precedent in the Catholic Church.

After four sessions, the Council Fathers approved the statements about the Jews in the document called *Nostra Aetate*. The deficiencies of the document were transparently clear at the time it was issued. And the Jewish community was quick to react by indicating what those shortcomings were. It was noted that the document did not use the term "condemn" in terms of anti-Semitism; it never employed the word "deicide." More significantly, the document does not have anything to say about contemporary Jewish reality—the current situation of the Jewish people and the people's current self-understanding. The Holocaust is not mentioned as such. The existence of the State of Israel seems scrupulously ignored. Nor did *Nostra Aetate* call for an end to missionary activity among the Jews. These omissions were greatly disappointing to the Jewish world. They seemed to bespeak a fundamental lack of appreciation of Jewish realities, or an indifference to central concerns of Jewish life as understood by Jews themselves.

At the time, the Jewish community was clearest in its statement of regret at what was not in the statement and in its expression of sadness that it was not stronger. It has been suggested by some that had the statement just emerged without any preliminary consultation, without Jews' being engaged in the process, they would have been elated with the statement. But since we were privy to the negotiations and to the ongoing give and take, there was the same feeling of mixed emotions that everybody has in the midst of a compromise. In such a circumstance you feel gratified at what you have achieved and yet at the same time, you still feel sadness in what you did not get. That, I think, is part of what the Jewish community felt at that time.

I also think, looking back, that there was a certain naiveté in Jewish expectation. The Catholic Church is an institution. Institutions do not make radical changes. No document issued by an official body is going to represent the extreme positions of members of that body. It will be a centrist statement, representing an establishment point of view. Jewish thinkers twenty years ago needed to remember that *Nostra Aetate* was a Catholic document, expressed in Catholic idiom, focusing on Catholic concerns, representing a consensus of the Catholic Church.

But, there were also other voices twenty years ago. I would like to share with you what Joseph Lichten said at the conclusion of the conference. He took a more temperate view:

> Now that the historic fourth session meeting has ended, in its effort to realize that the doctrines they propounded were the best which were possible in consideration of all the influences present—influences of cultural context, races, nationality, social concept and, most important, the religious legacy—from this viewpoint, the declaration on non-Christian religions, whatever its shortcomings, emerges as a milestone in the history of the Church.[3]

NOSTRA AETATE AS A SYMBOL

Let us move to a second major point. *Nostra Aetate* is not so important in what it said or did not say. The document is important as a symbolic watershed. The Catholic Church is undergoing major redefinition in many areas, including its relation to the Jews.

What *Nostra Aetate* did, whether it used the term "deicide" or not, was to radically redefine the character of the Catholic perception of the Jews. It put the Church officially on record as acknowledging the Jewish root of Christianity. And it put the Church officially on record as understanding the life and the ministry of Jesus in the context of the Jewish people. *Nostra Aetate* rejected supersessionism. It recognized the continuing existence of the Jewish people and acknowledged the vitality of Jewish religion. And it recognized the Jewish people and their faith as having an on-going place in God's design. That is a radical and a major change.

The Jewish people were no longer objects *de jure* of pity, of scorn, or of contempt. The basis for theological anti-Semitism had been extirpated. More important than that is what the document opened doors to. The document *Nostra Aetate* demands a new approach to understanding the New Testament. It required a new way of studying and of thinking about the Hebrew Scriptures, and it required of Catholics a more profound study of Jewish history. *Nostra Aetate* began a process—a process that does not always move forward so directly as we would like. It set forces in motion. Its end has not yet been seen.

What we celebrate, then, are the first fruits of *Nostra Aetate*, as well as the document itself. The later statements by bishops of various nations, including especially America and France, *did* come to terms with the Church's accountability for the Holocaust and with the central role of the State of Israel in the self-understanding of the Jewish people. The subsequent "Guidelines"—issued in 1975—*did* condemn anti-Semitism. And the study paper by Tomaso Federici *did* argue against missions to the Jews or evangelizing the Jews. Those are all developments which would have been impossible without *Nostra Aetate* and which were all enabled by its inactment.

And we have seen changes of a more immediate nature—changes that touch the lives of people: modifications of the liturgy, elimination of reproaches, a new approach to the reading of the gospels especially at times like Holy Week, shared revulsion at the depiction of the Jews as Christ killers, and the dropping of barriers of contact between Catholics and Jews.

Nostra Aetate began this as-yet-incomplete process. *Nostra Aetate* is essentially the posing of a question that is yet to be fully answered, though the answers have begun to come into focus. *Nostra Aetate* required a whole new theology of the Jews by the Catholic Church—who we are, what is our role in God's design, what is to be made of the fact that we did not accept Jesus as Messiah and still seem to be very much a part of God's scheme. *Nostra Aetate* itself did not propose such a theology. But it made the eventual articulation of that theology inescapable. It demanded of the future the wrestling with that question and the struggling towards its answer.

When that theology is expressed, it will find its first articulation in the wilderness, from the periphery, on the margins of the Church. Then it will come to be embraced by more and more established spokesmen. And only later, only when it is already accepted as common knowledge, will that theology become an article of faith articulated by the most official forum.

I believe it is of importance to discern what lay behind *Nostra Aetate*—what factors demanded that it be written. Its name *Nostra Aetate* identifies it as a document "of this age;" clearly it was precipitated by the events of this age.

Regardless of what the document does or does not say about it, the preeminent reality behind its composition was the *Shoah*, the Holocaust. Whether the Church could bring itself to say the words or not, it recognized the role of Church teaching in sowing the seeds of that destruction. To Jews, the sense of urgency felt for the enactment of *Nostra Aetate* certainly came from the *Shoah*. Jews of European background have an especially keen sense of the role of the Catholic Church in determining the fate of the Jews. And so they turned to that Church to assure that such an evil would not be perpetrated again, and that atonement somehow could be made.

It is instructive that Raul Hilburg, in his magisterial documentation of the Holocaust, *The Destruction of European Jewry*, begins his whole discussion with a long disquisition on theological anti-Semitism, beginning with the earliest Church council.

If the *Shoah* clearly lies behind *Nostra Aetate*, so does the rebirth of the State of Israel. Whether *Nostra Aetate* explicitly deals with it or not, the Church had to struggle to come to terms with what Emil Fackenheim has called "the Jewish return to history." The Jewish people was no longer a pariah people forced to wander in a kind of phantom life over the face of the earth. Now they were at home. For religious people, Jews and non-Jews alike, that return after two thousand years of dispersion raises a profound puzzle. If we believe that God acts in history, what can it mean that He would enact such a thing? What can God have in mind to bring that people back home? And everyone—Christians, Jews, and Muslims—must ask, "If exile was a punishment for the rejection of Jesus, what can the return mean?" And that accounts for the political nature of some of the give and take on the issues that I already have discussed.

A third cause, which I mentioned briefly before, is the ongoing contact on a human level that Jews and Catholics have enjoyed in the contemporary world. We no longer live isolated from one another, and so we have to make sense of our living together. That circumstance is especially pressing in the American scene. Jews and Catholics shared a common social-economic reality as this century began: two immigrant communities, two minority religious groups struggling to maintain their identity. I believe that is the major reason why the American Bishops were among the most progressive on this issue and resonated so keenly with Jewish perceptions.

The greatest issue of all, with which *Nostra Aetate*—and

frankly all of Vatican II—attempted to grapple, was the reality of secularism. Certainly in *Nostra Aetate*, the statement on the Jews and on non-Christian religions in general, is an attempt to come to terms with that phenomenon. Twenty years ago, before the emergence of the Moral Majority and such groups, it appeared as if the world was increasingly rendering both of our religious perspectives irrelevant. There was an implicit recognition by people of faith that we have more in common with one another, despite doctrinal differences, than we may have with secular people, people guided only by materialist concerns. So we had to find a way of accommodating to one another, of sharing those overarching perceptions, despite the ideological chasms.

One last point. "When will Jews acknowledge that they have something to gain as well as something to give from the dialogue?" I think that we have seen in the wake of *Nostra Aetate* a rush of dialogue between Jews and Catholics, and something of a diminishing of dialogue between Jews and Protestants, which is puzzling. Henry Siegman has articulated the notion of an asymmetry in the dialogue—the notion that while Christians have a *theological* need to understand Jews, Jews have a *political* need that Christians understand them, as it were. To put it more starkly, there is a theological impetus behind Christian involvement in dialogue, a political impetus behind Jewish involvement in dialogue.

I would like to amend the Siegman hypothesis and add a corollary. Jews *think* that their need is political, or, stated another way, the Jewish need is political *on one level*, but we have a *theological* need as well. We, too, need the benefit of the Christian reflection on our situation so as to fully understand our situation. And more deeply, only by engaging in conversation with one another do we come to understand ourselves. We recognize our differences and we need to have our differences thrown into highlight to understand ourselves. Furthermore, by talking to people of other spiritual angles, we sharpen our own spiritual insights. By looking into other religious traditions, with a sensitivity, though not with acquiescence, we come to recognize aspects of our own spirituality that we might have otherwise overlooked. By talking to the other, each of us may hear some aspect of our own tradition which is played in a minor key, which we had not heard before. Now we can hear it more clearly by virtue of hearing its resonance in the religious life of the other. Christians gain by talking to Jews perhaps some appreciation of what they too often caricature as law or structure. And Jews seem to gain some deeper sensitivity to the emotive component of religious life. That is present in our religious tradition, too, but perhaps not seen with the same acuity. So we are all enriched by this discussion between our two communities which was enabled only by the promulgation of this document twenty years ago.

I learned, in reflecting on this whole process, the importance of the holy diplomacy that Joseph Lichten, Thomas Stransky, and others were engaged in twenty years ago. It is all too easy for others in the Jewish community to deride it as an obsessive attention to minute and irrelevant details that are really of no value.

The role of the Jewish community in shaping *Nostra Aetate* underscores the need for this kind of holy diplomacy, for people whose work is eternal vigilance and for punctilious attention to the minutiae. All of the good that has come in these twenty years was possible only because people attended to that diplomacy and attended to the jots and tittles of this document as it was evolving.

That fruits of *Nostra Aetate* have been less bountiful than one might have expected is due perhaps to a strange twist of fate which Michael Signer pointed out to me. It is a sad paradox, a perversion of Kierkegaard's dialectical movement, if you will, that at the very moment the Church was reaching out to the Jewish community, the

Jewish community was pulling inward. The document, promulgated in 1965, preceded by only two years the Six-Day War. In the wake of what we perceived as Christian unresponsiveness to our disquiet and anxiety about that potential tragedy, Jews simply "closed down shop" in terms of reaching out. Our enthusiasm for interfaith dialogue waned, and we commenced a period of more private devotion to promoting our own welfare and security. It may be that that phase is now ending, and that Jews are ready once more to resume the work of mutuality.

By way of summary, the document *Nostra Aetate* is not perfect, and the Jewish response was not fully understanding of the document nor reciprocal. Yet we must celebrate not a document, but a moment. In *The Caine Mutiny*, Herman Wouk uses the image of a massive door turning on a tiny ball bearing. The moment of *Nostra Aetate* twenty years ago was like that ball bearing. A whole movement, a whole world will never be the same again. *Nostra Aetate* did not culminate, but commenced, the process of monumental change. We have seen some of the fruits of that change, but we cannot even conceive what the end will be. The smallest inkling of that change has already touched the lives of millions. We cannot calculate how many millions more will have their lives benefitted by it.

NOTES

1. Theodor Herzl's Diaries, January 23–26, 1904.

2. For much of the historical description about the events of the Vatican Council, the author acknowledges his profound debt to Arthur Gilbert, *The Vatican Council and the Jews* (Cleveland, Ohio: World Publishing Company, 1968). Gilbert has done a monumental job in reporting the discussions, statements, and give-and-take inside and outside the official meetings, that resulted in the creation of *Nostra Aetate*.

3. Joseph L. Lichten, *The Catholic World*, vol. 202:212: pp. 361–362.

III
Twenty Years of Progress

7. *Speculum Concilii*:
Through the Mirror Brightly

MICHAEL A. SIGNER

Omnis mundi creatura, quasi liber et pictura, nobis est in speculum.

All creatures of the world, like a book or picture, are a mirror for us (Alan of Lille).

There is a rabbinic dictum that is well suited to our task in looking back at *Nostra Aetate*: "It is not incumbent upon you to complete the task, but neither are you free to desist from it altogether."[1] Present day reflection upon this document takes place in the very same spirit that has occasioned two previous meetings at the University of Notre Dame. The 1966 interfaith appraisal of Vatican II devoted a session to *Nostra Aetate*.[2] The 1977 meeting at Notre Dame that occasioned the volume *Toward Vatican III* had no reflection on Jewry within the life of the Church.[3]

The hiatus of twenty years, however, may be fortuitous. We have more experience of the new relationship mandated in the decree. Even the appraisal after the council would seem to indicate that there was some immediate disappointment, but there was cause for optimism. Thomas Stransky remarked that, "At no time did the drafters of the document presuppose that the brief treatment would please all Jews. The document is for Catholics and thus in itself is a humble admission and confession that the Church in the 1960s has need of an evaluation of the positive relationship to the Jews and must condemn anti-Semitism."[4] Even more indicative of that tension between disappointment and optimism were the words of Rabbi Abraham Joshua Heschel. In the discussion of Rabbi Marc Tannenbaum's paper, Rabbi Heschel stated prophetically, "This is not an unconditional document. It is, however, an important document. It is not the climax because the movement is greater than the Council."[5]

We now witness the ongoing fulfillment of Heschel's prophecy. Reading the documents collected by Helga Croner demonstrates that one synod of bishops after another made the spirit of the council explicit.[6] Anti-Semitism has been condemned; Judaism is a complete religion and part of the mystery of God's saving power; Jews are not to be objects of evangelization; their conversion is not a desideratum. The bishops in the United States have been in the vanguard both at the council and in subsequent years. Yet our work continues. The doors have been opened, but bridges remain to be constructed across the chasm of silence.

That chasm of silence may have occasioned the ambivalent Jewish reaction to the statements of the council. It is clear that a lack of fraternal relations brought about the cacophany of Jewish expressions in the wake of the council and to subsequent statements made by the Vatican and the bishops. I would propose that another factor also controls Jewish reactions to these statements. The Jewish community tends to respond to all statements about Jews by other groups from a political perspective. The agenda is set exclusively from the Jewish vocabulary of survival which means the protection of the Jewish people's physical being and security. Within that lexicon, religious views are often separated from political concerns. Abraham Joshua Heschel could transcend the moment precisely because he was so sensitive to the inextricable bond between religion and society. He responded to *Nostra Aetate* with the insight of a religious thinker who knew that the spirit was present at the council and would continue to move those who would follow.

Rabbi Heschel represented a minority position within the Jewish community. For all of its unified appearance, the Jewish community struggles toward unity. We have no hierarchy: there are no official spokespeople within American, Israeli, or world Jewry. Members of the Jewish community were in 1966, and remain in 1985, ignorant of the Catholic Church as a whole body, as an *Ecclesia Perigrinans*. It is even difficult for the Jewish community to appreciate that not all Christians are Catholics. Our failure to discriminate between various types of pronouncements within the Church often controls our reaction. It brings us to short-ranged vision and prevents our comprehension that the infrastructure of the Church supports a new approach to Jews that transcends the single document *Nostra Aetate*.

Let me draw an example from the seminary in which I teach. We had a luncheon last week with a professor from the local diocesan seminary. My students were totally unaware that there were any other constitutions of Vatican II aside from *Nostra Aetate*. We Jews may be a special interest group within the broad concerns of the Church, but we cannot build a relationship without comprehending the whole picture of the Church. *Nostra Aetate* is supported and complemented by constitutions on the liturgy, divine revelation, and religious freedom. Such a subtle change as the reintroduction of the reading from Hebrew Scripture in the Sunday Mass made possible the presence of Judaism within the day-to-day life of the Church. This single change provided an opportunity for homilists to represent Judaism in new ways and correct old wrongs. The constitution on bishops and the church, which allowed more responsibility for local bishops to set guidelines, has permitted specific suggestions for implementing improved relationships toward the Jewish community.

When the smoke blows away from the most recent statement by the Vatican Commission for Religious Relations with the Jews (June 24, 1985) entitled, "Notes on the Correct Way to Present Jews and Judaism in Preaching and Catechesis in the Roman Catholic Church," we will acknowledge together that Jews have been moved into two key concepts within the message of the Church: catachesis and preaching. We can argue that the commission might have used its previous informal method of consulting Jewish experts. It may be said that the commission "did not go far enough." I believe that is to miss the point. The document fixes our gaze at the very heart of the problem of Jewish-Catholic relations: How shall the mandate of Jesus *"Docete omnes gentes,"* ["teach all peoples"] (Matt. 28:19) be fulfilled with respect to the Jews? Even further, we might ask what has been the Jewish response to all of these statements with respect to its own attitudes about teaching and preaching about Catholics in these twenty years?

We might argue that the Jewish response has been to remain "totally other." The doors newly opened in 1966 have provided an opportunity for Catholics to enter the world of contemporary Judaism and to learn. We have been "gracious hosts." If the mandate of the Council Fathers to the Church was to condemn anti-Semitism and to reflect upon the "special patrimony of Judaism and the Church," we have been willing to act in a prophetic mode. Being "totally other" has enabled the Church to sharpen its self-critique and analysis. The misreadings and misunderstandings which I have just outlined have been helpful to Catholics in clarifying their positions.

However, I would counter this argument with the proposition that to be "totally other" may in the end be isolating and self-defeating. To be a gracious host does not mean to be a brother, sister, or friend. It may not even bring us to a true dialogue, for we shall never speak our own hearts; we will only be able to react to what is said to us. We may be able to speak to one another, but never move to dialogue. If Jacob and Esau are our biblical prototypes, we shall never be able to move to the resolution they experienced. But if Jews take *Nostra Aetate* to heart and we are willing to enter into dialogue, we may invite ourselves into the hall of some of the most creative religious discourse in the modern world.

Let me borrow an image from my own field of specialization, the medieval world. One of the favorite metaphors of medieval scholars was that of the mirror (*speculum*). Alan of Lille's *De Planctu Naturae* suggests the following image of the world as a mirror.

> *Omnis mundi creatura*
> *quasi liber et pictura*
> *Nobis est in speculum.*[7]

Alan's image is significant because our dialogue through the centuries has been on many levels. We have written texts (*liber*) and have created visual images (*pictura*) of one another. We have engaged one another in a variety of economic circumstances and classes. The medieval reader of Alan's text may have recalled the statement by Pope Gregory I that doctrine is communicated to the educated by written books and to the uneducated by pictures.[8]

If, as Alan of Lille suggests, all the world is a mirror, then we Jews and Christians may indeed reflect one another. When we are at our best with respect to our two traditions, we can see "through the glass darkly" the outlines of the other's tradition. As we recognize those outlines we come to see parts of ourselves that we might otherwise overlook.

By seeing the Church and the Synagogue as mirrors of one another we can visualize both the symmetry and asymmetry of our relationships through the ages. We can understand that we both live with a dialectical tension of inclusivity and exclusivity. The mirror may demonstrate that what is in the foreground in one tradition may be in the background of the other tradition—but not missing entirely. For example, we would no longer be able to say "salvation" is not a meaningful term to Jews; rather, we ought to attempt to understand how the concept of "salvation" is reflected in Judaism. The mirror image calls Jews to dialogue in addition to assisting the Church in purging itself of past prejudice. It calls upon both traditions to reflect before they teach.

SPECULUM MUNDI: THE MIRROR OF OUR WORLD

If a mirror could be the image of our future relationships, we might turn to what I would call *speculum mundi,* the "mirror of our world" in the past twenty years. In many ways we have been setting the foundations for a new mutuality in relationships. In his paper at the University of Notre Dame in 1966, Rabbi Marc Tannenbaum set an agenda which has come to fruition.[9] We have written, together and separately, critical commentaries on the New Testament that clarify the relationships between various groups in the first century. Scholarly commentaries by scholars such as Raymond Brown and commentaries for more popular audiences such as *Mark* by Philip Van Linden are chipping away at the previous misunderstandings.[10] The works of Jacob Neusner, Ellis Rivkin, and Samuel Sandmel have contributed to this body of literature from a Jewish perspective.[11] Graduate programs at Jewish, Christian, and non-sectarian institutions of higher learning carry forward this program. One ought not neglect the institutes on Jewish-Christian relations that occur in Europe founded by Clemens Thoma and Peter Von der Osten-Sacken, and the work of Jakob J. Petuchowski, who now fills the German Herder Catalogue with almost as many books as he has in America.[12]

In 1966 Rabbi Tannenbaum also suggested that Jews and Catholics make greater efforts to "do theology" together, and to fill in the blank pages in the history of relations between one another. Institutes for Judeo-Christian studies and university departments of religion and theology have proven fertile ground for this activity. The University of Notre Dame has sponsored institutes and conferences which have led to the publications of such books as *Liturgical Foundations of Social Policy in the Catholic and Jewish Traditions* or the volume on the Land of Israel in the Jewish tradition.[13] Paulist Press has also supported the publication of significant efforts at mutual understanding. One must certainly mention the efforts in this area by Father John Pawlikowski with his excellent survey, *What Are They Saying about Catholic-Jewish Relations* or the challenge of *Christology in the Light of Jewish-Christian Dialogue.*[14]

Historians have been working in the field of Jewish-Christian relations during the past twenty years. The efforts of James Parkes to present a more balanced view of the premodern period have been augmented. Father Edward Flannery and Father Edward Synan have presented new material in the area of Church history.[15] Jewish scholars such as Bernhard Blumenkranz, David Berger, and Kenneth Stow are enriching our picture of institutional and cultural interaction between Jews and Christians in the medieval period.[16] Uriel Tal has set before us a more nuanced picture of the nineteenth century.[17] A shift in the emphasis to a more wholistic view of the place of Jews within a particular culture is helping to bring about a reevaluation of previous historical writings.

In the past twenty years we have observed the sincere efforts made by the Catholic community to further the mandates of *Nostra Aetate* in the area of school textbooks and catachetical materials. In some of the high school textbooks that I have seen there is an excellent description of the strands of Judaism during the first century. The authors of these textbooks have removed references to the "punishment" of the Jews in their exile. Significant also is the move away from the language of supersession—that the Church as the New Israel has eclipsed the Israel of Hebrew Scripture.[18] If Catholic youngsters now harbor ill-will toward their Jewish neighbors, we will have to seek the cause outside of the realm of textbooks which have been written since Vatican II. Of course, I must qualify these "optimistic" remarks and add that they derive from my personal observations. They might be largely limited to North America.

Even the difficult question of the bond between Jews and the State of Israel has seen improvement since Vatican II. We have been trying to speak to one another with greater clarity. Some of John Paul II's more recent statements indicate that a more significant empathy has been developing. I think it is also significant that some American Catholic seminaries have developed programs in Israel for their candidates. As these programs allow seminarians to travel and speak with Israeli Jews, the students will have personal experience with this most difficult area between us.

Perhaps we might take another measure of developments since Vatican II. We mentioned earlier that the council had given greater powers to local bishops to implement its programs. Los Angeles has become a large population center for Catholics. My efforts in writing this paper have brought me to consider the Los Angeles archdiocese and its efforts to further better relations with the Jewish community.

For close to fourteen years the Los Angeles Priest-Rabbi dialogue has continued. It has been my privilege to participate for the past eleven years. We are a mixed group. Three of the rabbis who have been active are seminary professors (two Conservative, one Reform), and one of the priests has been a professor of Scripture at St. John's seminary. The remaining members are pastors of local churches and rabbis of synagogues. Our first significant project was Lenten Guidelines. The priests wrote commentaries on the Lenten Scriptural readings, and the rabbis acted as their sounding board. From this topic, we moved into theological reflection with one another which has resulted in two pamphlets: "Covenant or Covenants" and "A Notion of the Kingdom."[19] In the first pamphlet we simply printed the Jewish and Catholic statements seriatim. In "A Notion of the Kingdom" we printed each section with a Jewish view, a Catholic view, and then added "our common views." It is significant to note the move toward greater mutuality within the format of our printed documents.

From the Rabbi-Priest dialogue evolved an exchange program between the Hebrew Union College and St. John's Seminary. Vatican II's constitution on the formation of priests was instrumental in shaping the nature of the exchange. We were told that the seminarians at St. John's now lived in a very busy atmosphere with a great variety of outside speakers and with numerous occasions to participate in programs. They would not be likely to attend an evening speaker. This "business" was also part of Hebrew Union College-Los Angeles which is essentially a "commuter" school. We concluded that it would be best if one faculty member from each school would spend a day in the other seminary, lecturing in a single class or a series of classes. We also allowed for some informal activities. The program began with an exchange between Scripture courses (an HUC faculty member spoke in New Testament classes at St. John's; a St. John's faculty member spoke on Hebrew Scripture at HUC). Subsequent years have brought faculty members into courses on liturgy, homiletics, and theology. In addition to courses, we attend the liturgies at each seminary. This has brought priests into our weekday liturgy and Torah reading at Hebrew Union College, and rabbis to eucharist, liturgy of the hours, and blessing of the sacrament. When the professor of Scripture at St. John's took a year's sabbatical, he was replaced by a member of the Hebrew Union College faculty.[20]

Our Jewish and Catholic seminarians also participate in an interseminary retreat program sponsored by the National Conference of Christians and Jews. Here they meet with students at various Catholic and Protestant seminaries. A parallel development among members of seminary faculties is underway in Los Angeles. The purpose of the faculty gatherings is not to provide a forum for scholarly papers, but an occasion for reflection on the task of seminary education.

One of the new projects in Los Angeles involves the students at Hebrew Union College as interns in Catholic high schools. This program, funded by an interreligious activities foundation called Project Discovery, enables rabbinic and religious education students to spend four hours a week as teaching interns. They are supervised by a master teacher in the Catholic high school and by members of our faculty of religious education. Both students in the high schools and our own students remark about the transforming nature of the program. Our students go out to teach, and they end up being taught.[21]

I believe that the next twenty years of *Nostra Aetate* lie in this transformation of the individual Catholic or Jew. In a sense *Nostra Aetate* was (as Father Stransky indicated twenty years ago) and remains a document for Catholics. It is a mandate to move the Church in America away from anti-Semitism. We have been witness to great energy in these efforts. We have not eradicated prejudice and ill feeling, but the source of that prejudice has been revealed. The teachings of the Church have been so revised that there is less and less excuse to base anti-Semitism on ecclesiastical sanction. One might make the claim that what is needed is to continue with greater rigor. Twenty years have given us the outlines of a new relationship. During the next twenty years our mission is to communicate the outlines to the broadest possible audience.

Part of me agrees with this analysis. We need to continue to communicate the revised teachings of the Church on Jews and Judaism. The laity is in constant need of education on so many areas of the council. *Nostra Aetate* needs to be taught with all the new material we have developed. As the Church becomes more complex in its ethnic composition there is a need to teach about Jews and Judaism. Literal interpretation of the Gospel, particularly about the passion narrative, is still part of the tradition of these immigrants. The Marxist invective against the bourgeoise has often been a transparent code for "Jews." We will all agree that zealousness is necessary to fulfill the mandates of the spirit of the Council Fathers.

At the same time as I urge continued vigilance toward anti-Jewish misinterpretations of the Church tradition, I would like to share what for me is implicit in *Nostra Aetate*. In the fourth paragraph of the council document we read,

> Since the spiritual patrimony common to Christian and Jews is thus so great, this Sacred Synod wishes to foster and recommend that mutual understanding and respect which is the fruit above all of biblical and theological studies, and of brotherly dialogues."

As a Jew, I understand these words to be a call or an invitation to serious dialogue. Within that dialogue, if it is to succeed, I must be more than the "gracious host" which I described earlier in this paper. At their best, our traditions are mirrors of one another. We Jews can benefit from a deeper understanding of contemporary Catholicism just as Catholics can benefit from a more nuanced comprehension of contemporary Judaism. We are what Samuel Sandmel used to call "two living traditions"; the moment that we "freeze" the other tradition, we lose a chance to better understand ourselves and our "common spiritual patrimony."[22]

SPECULUM ANIMAE: THE MIRROR OF THE SOUL

Some areas of dialogue might produce important insights for both Jews and Catholics over the next twenty years. I would call them *speculum animae,* "the mirror of the soul." They are areas where careful listening as well as teaching may bring us to deeper self-understanding and permit us to communicate our own tradition better within the Jewish community.

The first area for fruitful dialogue is in the literature of religious education. Writers such as Thomas Groome, Gabriel Moran, and Mary C. Boys have shifted the ground of religious education from questions of application (How do we teach the Bible?) to questions of synthesis and analysis (Why do we teach the Bible? Who are we who teach the Bible? What is the connection between Bible, tradition, and the world in which we live?).[23] Serious reflection upon the connection between ways of knowing and objects of knowledge are essential for liberal Jews whose approach to life attempts to bridge Jewish tradition and the ways in which one can live in a modern pluralistic society. As Jews and Catholics we live in constant tension with our traditions. We know that these traditions are not a single strand but multiple strands wound tightly together to produce a firm anchor or

bond. Many Jews and Catholics feel distanced or alienated from that bond. I believe that together we can help
one another answer appropriate and productive questions in religious education for our lay people and our
clergy.

A second area for fruitful dialogue is theology. In the
past twenty years we have learned from one another.
Our focus has been in comprehending the enormity of
the Holocaust. It is appropriate that our theology should
have begun with the Holocaust, for it represents the
pinnacle of the evil that the Council Fathers wished to
remove. Part of the process of *Nostra Aetate*'s genesis lay
in the book of Jules Isaac, *The Teachings of Contempt*. To
speak of the Holocaust before Christians has been a
significant form of witness for Jews. It has raised our
appreciation for the value of narrating a life-story as a
significant religious act. However, to tell *only* the story of
the Holocaust is a distortion of the Jewish tradition in its
totality. It deprives us of our "living tradition."

Not all Jews will want to theologize with non-Jews.
There are many in the Jewish community who would
agree with David Berger that meaningful dialogue with
Christians can take place only on social issues for the
betterment of our world, and not on "theology."[24] Part of
this reluctance may derive from historical conditioning.
We have had only twenty years of the post-Vatican II
Church. Until that time we were objects of evangelization
and the beneficiaries of prayers for our conversion.
Many Jews continue to associate Christianity with vio-
lence and pogroms—even though it may never have
been part of their experience. Old myths die hard on
both sides. At the core of the Jews' reluctance is a linger-
ing fear that there is more Jewish identity which may be
lost in dialogue than gained. There are also those Jews
who believe that the asymmetry between Judaism and
Christianity relieves them from any need to dialogue
with Christians. To be a Christian, they would argue,

requires one to understand Hebrew Scriptures as the appropriate background for the New Testament. Judaism, by contrast, moves from Scripture to Rabbinic literature and there has no need to encompass a knowledge of other religious traditions. The survival of the Jewish people is uppermost in the minds of these Jews—and many of them remained convinced that their ancestors survived to the degree to which they stood apart from all other civilizations.[25] I will return to this historical perception below.

At present, I want to press on with a direction for dialogue for those who believe that our mutual encounter can be transforming. That transformation takes place not when we become "the other," but when we become more profoundly aware of our own gifts through dialogue with "the other." The task at hand seems to become one of "translation" and hermeneutics.

As traditional religions we have each developed our own language, our own approaches to the world. To a certain extent we are indeed prisoners of our language and metaphors. One of the most common responses in dialogue among Jews is, "But that's a Christian category, not a Jewish category. Jews have no language for that concept." With some efforts at translation we Jews can move into significant new areas which have received little attention. Eugene Borowitz's book, *Contemporary Christologies: A Jewish Response,* indicates that there is much to learn about religious anthropology from current discussion of Christology.[26] Abraham Joshua Heschel chided modern Jewish religious thinkers for their failure to develop a significant religious anthropology. When and if we read some of the current literature on this problem and probe its deepest structures, we can renew our search within the vastness of rabbinic literature and develop new answers. In the spirit of Hans George Gadamer's hermeneutics, we may learn new questions and thereby find new paths to the understanding of our own tradition.[27]

In my own Reform Jewish tradition there is, after 150 years of exclusive emphasis on rationalism and empiricism, a stirring of the spirit. Clergy and laity are reexamining the Jewish tradition in order to develop new resources for their own spirituality. I would like to think it is not accidental that the central lay board of Reform Judaism, the Union of American Hebrew Congregations, has passed a resolution on improved dialogue with Catholics. The Union of American Hebrew Congregations has also published a volume with the National Council of Catholic Bishops on Peace and Justice.[28] However, progress in Jewish-Catholic relations within the Reform movement is uneven. When I studied in religious school more than twenty-five years ago, we attended Christian worship with both Catholics and Protestants as part of our studies. My children attend that same synagogue school. They have not experienced any worship outside the Jewish environment. Study together must be augmented with positive experiences of how we celebrate our traditions. The rich tradition of individual spirituality within the Catholic Church can help us to find resources within our own Jewish tradition. The Paulist Press series has made available spiritual masters of the Jewish tradition such as Nachman of Bratzlav, Menachem of Chernobyl, and the Zohar. A study of spiritual masters such as Anselm of Canterbury might show us that *fides quaerens intellectum* (faith seeking understanding) is a dialectical relationship. *Fides* and *intellectum* are each categories worthy of consideration; one enriches the other, but need not diminish it.

The life-experience of Catholics in their quest for spirituality may also be a fruitful source for dialogue. Jews have not gone on retreats. There are Jewish camps, but no retreat houses. Rabbis and other professionals in the Jewish community have never sought renewal within these institutions. Yet there is an intuition that we have much to learn in this area. Prayer and reflection are very much part of the Jewish experience. Questioning and dialogue with Catholics will aid us in the urgency of recovering our contemplative tradition. The student sermons in our synagogue at the Hebrew Union College in Los Angeles about the need to develop a spirituality reveal that our seminary curriculum is in need of rethinking this part of our tradition. We are already planning a day of recollection with St. John's Seminary. It is my hope that this day will begin an important dialogue between our two faculties.

I am not suggesting that the Hebrew Union College transform itself into a center for priestly formation; nor would I want either Judaism or Catholicism to make itself over. There are significant differences that our traditions will continue to impose upon us. It will be difficult for Jews to translate Christological images and metaphors. It will be difficult for Catholics to translate the Rabbinic hermeneutical discussions of Scripture. However, each tradition will help one another to a new understanding of itself.

There is a third area for productive dialogue in the future. I believe that we need to broaden our understanding of our encounter through the centuries.[29] We would acknowledge that religious literature and human interaction reflect each other in a most oblique way. Religious literature is countercultural by its nature; it challenges reality and attempts to transform it. Careful examination of human interaction, which is the task of historians, has much to contribute to religious life.

We have seen how historical examination of the Christian roots of anti-Semitism quickened the spirit of the council twenty years ago. Historians scraped away and revealed that pious literature had produced bitter fruit. The writings of Gavin Langmuir and Leon Poliakov have revealed the insidious consistency of anti-Jewish teachings. Long after papal condemnation of blood-libels against the Jews, these trials continued.[30]

Our historical understanding of the first Christian century has deepened over the past twenty years. We

have a scholarly consensus that Pharisaic and Rabbinic
Judaism cannot be studied without a knowledge of all
available sources—New Testament, Mishnah, Midrash,
and Dead Sea Scrolls. The development of scholarly
research on Rabbinic Judaism is now reaching into the
world of the Church Fathers. Origen and the Rabbis are
being studied as part of the same cultural ambience.
There is still considerable resistance to this comparative
study from many Jewish colleagues. In some circles one
may still find those who believe that interdependence
diminishes sanctity. I do not believe that, and I would
hope that the Rabbis and Church Fathers will be studied
together.

To these efforts which focus on the "classical" periods
of the development of our tradition, I would hope that
we would move on to the medieval and modern period.
In order to accomplish this research we have to see the
history of Jewish-Christian relations as more than the
"vale of tears." Salo W. Baron decried the lachrymose
concept of Jewish history in the 1930s. However, it is this
ongoing dirge that many Jews find supportive of their
own identity. We ought to be asking different questions.
How did our ancestors address questions of reason and
revelation? How did they develop hermeneutical structures to bridge the gap between tradition and contemporary theological conflicts?

When these questions become a primary focus, our
concept becomes more nuanced and previously un-
noticed groups gain significance. An example of this
development may be the current interest in early scholas-
tic exegesis and theology. The School of St. Victor in
twelfth-century Paris, discovered by Father G. Lacombe
and Beryl Smalley, provides important evidence on hermeneutical questions and on Jewish-Christian relations.
The neo-Augustinian approach of Hugh of St. Victor
brought about a new synthesis of spirituality and learning. Letter and spirit within Scripture were brought into

dynamic tension instead of hierarchy and subordination. Once the letter gained in importance, Hebrew studies and dialogue with Jews became necessary. The "dialogue" at St. Victor did not reveal a post-Vatican II tolerance, but it does provide a significant historical precedent.[31] One might also cite Ivan Marcus's book, *Piety and Society: The Jewish Pietists of Medieval Germany*, as an example of the absorption of thirteenth-century Jews into their environment.[32] At the Sol and Arlene Bronstein Colloquium in Cincinnati, Hans Hermann Henrix utilized Franz Rosenzweig's model of "community/noncommunity" to describe the history of Jewish-Christian relations.[33] We have much to learn from the roads that we have travelled separately—but together.

SPECULUM HUMANAE SALVATIONIS: THE MIRROR OF HUMAN SALVATION

In conclusion, I would like to suggest yet another mirror image, *speculum humanae salvantionis* (the mirror of human salvation). *Nostra Aetate* is a declaration on non-Christian religions. The document represents the Church's attitude toward Islam, Hinduism, and Buddhism. This broad scope provides a most important context for paragraph 4 on Jews and Judaism.

Twenty years ago we knew that the European and North American bishops were most vitally concerned with a postive statement about Judaism. It is clear that the bishops of the Middle East were opposed to the statement throughout the council's deliberations. The bishops of Asia and Africa were, at best, indifferent.

As we celebrate *Nostra Aetate* in Europe and America we ought to acknowledge that the growth of the Church in Third World countries is quite remarkable. There has not been a presence of Jews in those countries. It may be that the absence of Jews may lead to simplistic readings of the Gospel or understandings of the liturgy which countenance anti-Judaism.

In countries where there has been development of liberation theologies, there does not seem to have been a concomitant integration of *Nostra Aetate*'s teachings about Jews and Judaism. The tools for societal analysis provided by Marxist teachings have given rise to anti-Jewish sentiments in Western European countries. Without the vigilant recollection of *Nostra Aetate,* we may observe the growth of anti-Jewish *animus* in new areas.

This final mirror indicates how significant our presence has become to one another. When Jews and Catholics move apart from each other, the opportunities for distortion grow. A Catholic may study Jewish texts in isolation from Jews, but those texts receive an entirely new meaning when studied in the presence of Jews. Similarly, Jews may study about Christianity and its literature, but a profoundly different experience occurs when we study together. Dialogue implies our willingness to listen to one another and learn together without immediately dissecting the experience and creating polar opposites. In the presence of one another we may have the encounter. We might then retire to isolation to evaluate the meaning of the encounter. When we come to study together again we will have allowed the dialogue to transform us. This transformation in self-understanding would seem to comport with the Rabbinic dictum, "Provide yourself with a teacher, and acquire a friend."[34] We may come to dialogue to teach, but our goal is profound human companionship in the experience of our world as religious beings.

A final mirror image emerges from Rabbinic literature to describe the future of our dialogue. The Rabbis contrasted the earthly king with the divine sovereign. An earthly king set his image on a coin, and the same image is stamped on each coin. The divine sovereign stamps the image of the first man on each human being, and yet each human being is unique.[35] When we are fully present to one another in dialogue our unique selves are revealed in the divine image. Our task lies before us with the urgency suggested by Rabbi Tarfon, "The day is short; the work is great, and the Master of the House is pressing."[36]

NOTES

1. Mishnah, *Avot* 2:16.

2. John H. Miller, ed., *Vatican II: An Interfaith Appraisal* (Notre Dame, Ind.: University of Notre Dame Press, 1966), pp. 316–374.

3. David Tracy, ed., *Toward Vatican III: The Work that Needs to be Done* (New York: Crossroad, 1978).

4. J. Miller, *Vatican II*, pp. 373–374.

5. Ibid.

6. Helga Croner, *Stepping Stones to Further Jewish-Christian Relations* (New York: Paulist, 1977), and *More Stepping Stones to Jewish-Christian Relations* (New York: Paulist, 1985).

7. Alan of Lille, *De Planctu Naturae.*

8. Gregory I, *Ep. "Literarum tuarum primordia" ad Serenum episc. Massilinensum,* Oct. 600 in Denziger and Schonmetzer, *Enchiridon Symbolorum* (New York: 1963), p. 477.

9. J. Miller, *Vatican II*, p. 366.

10. Some examples of the extensive writings of Father Brown which shed new light on Jewish-Christian relations are: *The Gospel According to John: A New Translation with Introduction and Commentary,* 2 vols., Anchor Bible, Nos. 29–29a; *Antioch and Rome: New Testament Cradles of Catholic Christianity* (New York: Paulist, 1983) (with John Meier); *New Testament Essays* (New York: Paulist, 1968). Philip van Linden, C.M., *Knowing Christ through Mark's Gospel,* Herald Biblical Booklets, (Chicago: Franciscan Herald, 1976), presents some excellent material for lay-reflection about issues pertinent to Jewish-Christian dialogue.

11. Each of these authors has been prolific in their contribution both the scholarly and popular literature relating to

Jewish-Christian relations. I present here only a single example of their writings. Jacob Neusner, *Judaism in the Beginnings of Christianity* (Philadelphia: Fortress, 1984). Ellis Rivkin, *A Hidden Revolution* (Nashville, Tenn.: Abingdon, 1978). Samuel Sandmel, *The First Century in Judaism and Christianity: Certainties and Uncertainties* (Oxford: Oxford University Press, 1969).

12. Clemens Thoma, *A Christian Theology of Judaism* (New York: Paulist, 1980). Peter von der Osten-Sacken, *Katechismus und Siddür Aufbruche mit Martin Luther und Lehrern Israels* (Berlin: Institut Kirche und Judentum, 1984). For an extensive bibliography of literature about Jewish-Christian dialogue in Germany, see Hans Hermann Henrix, "The Aims and Objectives of Judaeo-Christian Studies—A Christian View," in J. Petuchowski, ed., *Defining a Discipline: The Aims and Objectives of Judaeo-Christian Studies Papers Presented at the First Bronstein Colloquium, November 7–8, 1983* (Cincinnati, Ohio: Hebrew Union College, 1984), pp. 39–72.

13. Daniel Polish and Eugene J. Fisher, eds., *Liturgical Foundations of Social Policy in the Catholic and Jewish Traditions* (Notre Dame, Ind.: University of Notre Dame Press, 1983), and Lawrence A. Hoffman, ed., *The Land of Israel: Jewish Perspectives* (Notre Dame, Ind.: University of Notre Dame Press, 1986).

14. John Pawlikowski, *What Are They Saying about Christian-Jewish Relations* (New York: Paulist, 1980); *Christ in the Light of the Christian-Jewish Dialogue* (New York: Paulist, 1982).

15. James Parkes, *The Conflict of the Church and the Synagogue* (Cleveland, Ohio: World Publishing, 1961); *The Jew in the Medieval World,* 2nd ed. (New York: Hermon Press, 1976). Edward Flannery, *The Anguish of the Jews* (New York: Macmillan, 1965). Edward A. Synan, *The Popes and the Jews in the Middle Ages* (New York: Macmillan, 1965).

16. Bernhard Blumenkranz, *Juifs et Chrétiens dans le monde occidental* (Paris: Mouton, 1960). David Berger, *The Jewish-Christian Debate in the High Middle Ages* (Philadelphia: Jewish Publication Society, 1979). Kenneth Stow, *Catholic Thought and Papal Policy* (New York: Jewish Theological Seminary of America, 1976).

17. Uriel Tal, *Christians and Jews in Germany: Religion, Politics, and Ideology in the Second Reich. 1870–1914* (Ithaca, N.Y.: Cornell University Press, 1975).

18. Eugene J. Fisher, *Faith Without Prejudice* (New York: Paulist, 1977). John Pawlikowski, *Catechetics and Prejudice* (New York: Paulist, 1983).

19. The pamphlets may be obtained from the office of the Southern California Board of Rabbis, 6505 Wilshire Boulevard, Los Angeles, California 90048.

20. A pamphlet describing the history and focus of the HUC-St. John's Exchange was published by St. John's and may be obtained from the Seminary at 5012 E. Seminary Road, Camarillo, California.

21. The project is financed by "Project Discovery," an amalgam of activities whose impetus comes from Rabbi Alfred Wolf and Rev. Msgr. Royale Vadakin of Los Angeles, California. Most of the activities mentioned in this section of the article have their origins in the creative synergy of Rabbi Wolf and Msgr. Vadakin. Their continued dedication to furthering interreligious understanding will no doubt lead to further projects in Los Angeles.

22. Samuel Sandmel, *Two Living Traditions: Essays on Religion and the Bible* (Detroit: Wayne State University Press, 1972).

23. Thomas Groome, *Christian Religious Education* (San Francisco: Harper and Row, 1980). Gabriel Moran, *Education toward Adulthood: Religion and Lifelong Learning* (New York: 1974). Mary C. Boys, "Questions which Touch on the Heart of Our Faith," in *Religious Education* 76:6 (Nov.-Dec. 1981), pp. 636–656.

24. David Berger, "Jewish-Christian Relations. A Jewish Perspective," in *Journal of Ecumenical Studies* 20:1 (1983): pp. 5–32.

25. An excellent summary of "roadblocks" for Jews on the way to dialogue with Christians is to be found in *Homework for Jews: Preparing for Jewish-Christian Dialogue*, 2nd ed., by Janet Sternfeld, *National Conference of Christians and Jews* (1985).

26. Eugene Borowitz, *Contemporary Christologies: A Jewish Approach* (New York: Paulist, 1980).

27. Hans Georg Gadamer, "The Universality of the Hermeneutical Problem," in *Philosophical Hermeneutics* (Berkeley, Calif.: University of California Press, 1977), pp. 3017.

28. Annette Daum and John Pawlikowski, *Shalom: the Challenge of Peace* (New York: Union of American Hebrew Congregations, 1985).

29. Salo W. Baron, "Emphasis in Jewish History," in *Jewish History and Historians* (Philadelphia: Jewish Publication Society, 1964), pp. 65–89. Yosef Haim Yerushalmi, *Zakhor: Jewish History and Jewish Memory* (Seattle: University of Washington Press, 1982) provides an excellent reflection on the relationship between Jewish history and Jewish identity.

30. Gavin Langmuir, "Prolegomenon to any Present Analysis of Hostility against Jews," in *Social Science Information* 15:4/5 (1976): pp. 689–727. Leon Poliakov, *History of Anti-Semitism*, 3 Vols. (New York: Vanguard Press, 1965).

31. On the Victorine school of biblical exegesis one should consult Beryl Smalley, *The Study of the Bible in the Middle Ages*, 3rd ed. (Oxford: Basil Blackwell, 1984). Andrew of St. Victor's utilization of Jewish sources will be described in my edition of his commentary on Ezekiel which will appear in *Corpus Christianorum Continuatio Medievalis* as part of volume 53.

32. Ivan G. Marcus, *Piety and Society: The Jewish Pietists of Medieval Germany* (Leiden: E.J. Brill, 1981).

33. See above, note 12.

34. Mishnah, *Avot* 1:6.

35. Mishnah, *Sanhedrin* 4:5 (paraphrase).

36. Mishnah, *Avot* 2:15.

8. Seminaries, Classrooms, Pulpits, Streets: Where We Have to Go

EDWARD FLANNERY

> To look at these few years across the millenia that
> preceded them, they are, admittedly, the most satis-
> fying and heartening in all of Jewish-Christian history.
> But viewed in the short run and in the light of the
> enormity of the debt we as Christians have inherited
> from an alienated past and the consequent enormity of
> the task of reparation and reconstruction that lies
> ahead, how can we see them but as faltering and
> slothful?

Considered in itself, paragraph 4 of *Nostra Aetate* is not an
impressive document. Too brief for its important purpose; inserted, despite Christianity's unique relation to
Judaism, between eulogies of Hinduism and Buddhism
and professions of respect for all humankind; and to a
certain degree compromised by intermural struggles
over its substance and composition, it falls far short of the
strong and ringing statement it could have been. But
considered in its circumstance and viewed historically, it
is impressive. Despite flaws and diminutive stature, it
looms large on the pages of religious history. Few documents of any size or of whatever content have so rapidly
revolutionized in a positive direction the relations of two

faith-traditions. Terminating in a stroke a millenial teaching of contempt of Jews and Judaism and unequivocably asserting the Church's debt to its Jewish heritage, it represents an epoch-making reversal, a leap into a new dimension of Jewish-Christian relations. Few such revolutions have ennobled the pages of Christian history.

What accounts for the contrast between text and circumstance in the destiny of this document? The reception it received accounts for the difference. *Nostra Aetate,* in other words, became impressive in its sequel, in its effects. For in its wake came a rich growth of Jewish-Christian dialogue, the breaking of a centuries-old silence. Certainly this dialogue has been one of the most notable emergences on the ecumenical scene.

Twenty years have now passed since this remarkable dialogical flowering began, and a wealth of experience has accumulated. It is my task in this paper, in the light of that experience, to evaluate the developments of this score of years from a Catholic perspective. Such an evaluation poses a problem. Is there a Catholic perspective? I prefer to refer to my observations and reflections as: "a" Catholic's perspective; in other words, my own, which, it is to be hoped, will approximate the position of most Catholics in the not too distant future. But we must recognize that the last twenty years are the product of the near two thousand that preceded them. Anyone who knows anything about those two millenia will know why we should first ask the Jews what these last twenty years have been and what they have accomplished. The debt accruing from the estrangement of our mutual past rests almost entirely on the Christian side. It is too early for the Christian to expect or ask for reciprocity in our dialogues or programs. It would seem a Christian thing to adopt the Jewish agenda *tout court.*

THE ISSUES OF THE DIALOGUE

It is a commonplace in the Jewish-Christian colloquium that Christians want to talk theology while Jews
prefer to talk about humanitarian and historical realities,
more especially, anti-Semitism, the Holocaust, and the
State of Israel, which for Jews are life and death issues. I
might add here that Jews, sensitive to Christian wishes,
do not always press for or suggest some of these subjects—a state of affairs that should encourage Christians
to take the initiative in their regard. To my mind, there
are four foremost issues of the dialogue: (1) the revision
of the traditional Christian theology of Judaism, (2) anti-
Semitism, (3), the Holocaust, and (4) Israel. What we
have achieved in dealing with them will provide the standard for judging the fruitfulness or progress of the last
twenty years. It is understood, to be sure, that there are
other subjects and agenda for our dialogues and other
ways of Jewish-Christian cooperation, but they should
not enjoy the priority or be conceded the time and energy that is given to these four paramount issues.

The priority one grants to subjects or agenda of dialogue depends, of course, upon one's concept of the
ultimate aim of that dialogue. This aim is often defined
as mutual understanding of Christians and Jews, but this
concept appears to me somewhat elitist, making our coming together mostly a cognitive enterprise, a task for
scholars. It assuredly should be this, but is it enough? If
we view the Jewish-Christian problem historically,
whether as to the past or the present, it comes forth as an
alienation of two peoples, Jewish and Christian, both
millions strong. In this context, the final goal of the
dialogue is the reconcilation of the Jewish and Christian
peoples, considered in their entirety. For this reason any
method or measure enlisted in the Jewish-Christian encounter that is not turned in an effective way toward this
massive reconciliation is deficient and fails to recognize
the seriousness and magnitude of the task before us.

A REVISION OF TRADITIONAL CHRISTIAN THEOLOGY

How have these four critical issues fared since the issuance of *Nostra Aetate*? Let us turn to the theological issue, not because it is of first importance, but because *Nostra Aetate* is primarily a theological document. Furthermore, even if theological discussions are not the primary requisite of the dialogue, they are nonetheless essential, and for three reasons. First, there is no other way for two faith-traditions with such close ties to understand one another, and in the case of Christianity, with its genetic ties to Judaism, to understand itself. Second, Christian anti-Semitism took root in Christian theology and to some degree is still nourished by it today; its elimination hence can hardly be fully achieved without some theological revision. Third, although this revision is a task incumbent on Christian theologians, it is one that cannot be brought to a successful end without the aid and resources of Jewish theologians and scholars.

The need for revision received a vigorous impetus from *Nostra Aetate*'s recommendation that Catholics and Jews engage in "biblical and theological studies, and . . . brotherly dialogue."[1] The process was already given major contributions in the document's rejection of the age-old deicide charge leveled against the Jewish people throughout the centuries with such devastating consequences, and in its affirmation of Judaism's retention *post Christum* of its covenants and promises. The next major advance came ten years later in the Vatican's "Guidelines and Suggestions for Jewish-Christian Relations." This document, a practical one, offered little theology but enunciated a principle of crucial theological significance, which stated that "Christians must strive to learn by what essential traits the Jews define themselves in the light of their own religious experience." The days of Christians defining Judaism or Jewry for Jews as well as for Christians was over; but, as we shall see, little did the Church know at the time how difficult it might be at times to abide by that principle. In a way the Vatican had preempted its implementation of the principle when in the previous year (1974) it created a Vatican Commission for *Religious* Relations with Jews. It was made clear both by the title and meetings of the Commission that the subject of Israel, so central to Jewish religious as well as ethnic or political self-understanding, was barred from discussion as a political matter, and therefore not fitting fare for religious theological discussions.

The recent "Notes on the Correct Way to Present Jews and Judaism in Preaching and Catechesis in the Roman Catholic Church" (1985),[2] issued by the same Commission, offered many theses and reflections of importance for Catholic and Jewish understanding, several of which were unquestionably advances. The Holocaust and Israel, for example, were mentioned for the first time in a Vatican document, but in a most restrictive manner. On the whole, it is difficult to see this document as genuine progress; indeed some observers have seen it as stasis; and many Jews and some Catholics deeply involved in the dialogue have seen it as regress. To keep our judgment in perspective it would be well to bear in mind Dr. Eugene Fisher's observations that, in some areas where the dialogue is not so advanced, the "Notes" will be seen as a "blockbuster" by reason of its positive statements about Jews and Judaism. The most serious problem with the "Notes" may finally be that of their implementation. If they suffer the fate of other ecclesial documents on Jewish-Christian relations they may well be destined for an early grave on ecclesial shelves, unacted upon.

For further progress in the project of revision, recourse must be made to Catholic revisionist theologians, some of whom drew their first inspiration from *Nostra Aetate*. I restrict my remarks to Catholic theologians and scholars, because *Nostra`Aetate* had them primarily in mind and, besides, I do not feel competent to assess whatever influence this document has had upon Protestant theologians. I do not believe it has been considerable. If I might hazard a comparison of Catholic and Protestant theology in this respect I would say that conservative Protestant theological opinion is more fundamentalist than the Catholic right, and liberal Protestant opinion more radical than the Catholic left. The Protestant spectrum is, in short, a wider one.

From the Catholic scene a sizable and growing list of these theologians can be drawn. It is possible to distinguish two groups: an original group that for some years has deeply committed itself to the task of theological revision. Such names readily come to mind as John Pawlikowski, John Oesterreicher, Marcel Dubois, Monica Hellwig, Eva Fleishner, Gregory Baum, Rosemary Ruether, Kurt Hruby, Charlotte Klein, Clemens Thoma, and Franz Mussner, and there are others. Another small group less involved includes systematic theologians of wide renown among Christian theologians generally—Hans Küng, Edward Schillebeeckx, Johannes Metz, and in this country, David Tracy. It is safe to say that for the rest, mainstream Catholic theologians have tended to give the subject of Jewish-Christian theology a wide berth.[3] Yet, even among them, *Nostra Aetate* has created a climate in which interest in this subject has grown and doubtless will continue to do so.

What has been the result of the theological effort? Has a new theology of Judaism or of the relationship of Judaism and Christianity emerged? Has a consensus been formed? The objective these theologians have set for themselves is the correction and emendation of Christian theology aiming to excise as far as possible the anti-Judaic elements of traditional teachings and to accord Judaism its proper theological validity and importance from a Christian perspective. Thus far a degree of consensus has materialized. Virtually all agree that any Christian theological consideration of Judaism must include a full appreciation of the Jewish heritage of Christianity, the Jewishness of Jesus and the primitive Church; the rejection of offensive teachings such as the deicide accusation and the divine repudiation and replacement of Judaism; invidious comparisons of Christianity with Judaism, and repudiation of anti-Semitism as sinful and un-Christian. The thesis that Jesus need not be seen as the Jewish Messiah, or in any case did not fulfill all Messianic expectations of Judaism, but rather that He is the Messiah or Christ of the Gentiles, tends to approach a consensus. Beyond this, consensus tends to disappear.

Opinions diverge in two directions. Most theologians who work in this area of research generally take a liberal or progressive turn and call for a reconsideration of traditional Christology as central to the problem of anti-Judaic theology. The problem they confront here is that of reconciling the uniqueness of Christianity while "making room," so to say, for Judaism's perpetual validity in the divine plan. Rosemary Ruether in particular has had the merit of pressing the theological dialogue vigorously in this direction and has catalyzed a rich outgrowth of creative theologizing on the relationship of Judaism to Christianity—often in reactive opposition to her views. Ruether sees anti-Judaism (which, she believes, inevitably leads to anti-Semitism) as essential to traditional Christology, its "left hand," as she terms it; and she posits a direct ideological as well as historical line from Christian anti-Semitism to modern racist anti-Semitism, as exemplified by the Nazi regime in our own time.[4] Most respondents have found her theses too radical and unnecessary and have sought more moderate positions that do not cut so closely to the heart of traditional Christology.

On the other side of the present theological effort stand more conservative theologians and thinkers who eschew all alterations of Christology and limit their revisions to the contents of the aforementioned consensus.

Basic to their thinking is the assurance that anti-Semitism is not inherent to Christianity or traditional Christology and that the consolidation of Jewish-Christian friendship and understanding can be achieved on the basis of Christian ethics and interpersonal harmony. They consider Christological revision an accommodation that no dialogue can require.[5]

Can these diverging directions of the theological dialogue be mediated and narrowed? At present, among Catholic theologians Christological revision appears to situate itself within what we might call a "liberal consensus" that finds strong support among mainstream Protestant theologians who interest themselves in the dialogue. The more conservative consensus has firm evangelical Protestant backing. The prospect that a centrist consensus shaped from these two poles of theological thought will mature in the near future is not a promising one. The question of importance now is whether the existing consensus can be consolidated and widened. More importantly, we must ask whether the resultant theological product will recommend itself to the generality of recognized systematic theologians and in this way bring a decisive influence to bear on the official church in its formulations of teachings, policies, and guidelines concerned with Jewish-Christian relations. Only thus will scholarly research on the subject, so zealously pursued these twenty or more years, finally find its way into the seminaries, classrooms, and pulpits of the churches and achieve the ultimate goal of our efforts—the reconciliation of the Christian and Jewish peoples.

Recently, I had the happiness of returning to Israel and meeting Marcel Dubois, a Dominican priest and long-time practitioner of the Jewish-Christian dialogue, and David Flusser, renowned Jewish New Testament scholar. Both are participants in the Interfaith Committee and the Rainbow group, two Jewish-Christian dialogue groups of long standing—groups that seem to have reached a stage of dialogue not as yet experienced in this country. Dubois posed the question of Jesus as a "stumbling block and unifier" of Christians and Jews—a subject I have not heard discussed here. This question, it must be understood, has nothing to do with the question of conversion of Christians or Jews. Flusser's response to Dubois was: "Jesus is my Master, He is your Lord." Apparently the reclamationist movement, as it is often called, according to which Jews would reclaim Jesus as a major Jewish prophet, is further advanced in Israel than elsewhere. Hearing of Flusser's remark, the question arose in my mind: Is this an intimation of things to come, a new stage of dialogue beyond revision, a dialogue *en famille,* in which brothers and sisters disagree but are as comfortable in their disagreement as they are in their agreement?

Possibly. But, be this as it may, for the moment we must continue our revisionist efforts. It is not for Jewish-Christian harmony alone that Christian dialogists work but for the integrity of Christian teaching as well. For all that, some questions may be placed on the primacy and proportions conceded to theological revisionism in the Jewish-Christian enterprise. In the Western world, in a secularized age, the relationship of the Church and the Synagogue no longer depends so much on theology, as in earlier times, but rather on personal, psychological, and sociological issues that impinge more on day-to-day human relationships of Christians and Jews. This is not said in an anti-intellectualist sense, but in light of the ultimate goal, the reconciliation of our peoples. My question is: Should not Christian as well as Jewish scholarship turn more of its energies to the exploration of what I might call life and death issues, such as the persistence of anti-Semitism, the Holocaust, the meaning and survival of Israel, the problem of secularism, the deficiencies of dialogue, and the like. It is in the direction of these that I now turn.

ANTI-SEMITISM

The subject that merits first priority in the Jewish-Christian colloquium is anti-Semitism. It is a priority that has been widely questioned, not only by Christians, but also by Jews, who, well aware of its presence and noxious influence on our mutual relations, are willing to forego its discussion for fear of irritating some Christians. Jews know of the Christian reluctance to confront the subject, but few Christians do. Perhaps in attempting to understand this reluctance we may best gain some insight into the importance and nature of the anti-Semitic phenomenon. In the final analysis, the reluctance derives from ignorance and unawareness—ignorance of the Christian anti-Semitic record, unawareness of the anti-Semitic presence in ourselves, and the resultant unawareness of its relevance and importance for the dialogue. Otherwise and simply stated, the reluctance is a failure to appreciate the magnitude of the anti-Semitic problem.

First, the anti-Semitic record and its magnitude. To my mind, anti-Semitism is the greatest hatred in human history. As to duration and recurrent intensity combined, there is nothing comparable to it. Granted, there are other hatreds that have surpassed it in fury for a while, but all of these (including anti-Black hatred in this country, for example) have their day and eventually disappear or assume the subdued level of customary popular biases. Not so anti-Semitism. Twenty-three centuries long, it has *survived* a genocide of six million of its victims in its twenty-third century of existence, only to find itself still very much alive with prospects of many years of life ahead.

I am aware that anti-Semitism is generally considered to be on the decline, at least in this country and at one of its lowest ebbs in history; some would say it is moribund. Against the position of Charles Silberman and those who agree with him, we should listen to Dr. Yehuda Bauer, chairperson of the International Center of Study of Anti-Semitism at Hebrew University in Jerusalem, who tells us it is on the rise again and deplores the apathy of Jews as well as Christians to this development. Or to James Parkes, of blessed memory, a life-long student of anti-Semitism, who some fifty years ago, when asked how long it would last, replied, "Three hundred years." It is mere wishful thinking to believe that we are in the last stages of this millenial malady—unless, of course, we resolutely step up our efforts in the war against it. But before that can occur it is necessary to *see* it: in our past, in the present, and in ourselves.

Few Christians have seen anti-Semitism in the text-books of Christian history, and for the simple reason that (with a few exceptions) it is still a missing page in our history books. Little do they know that Jews were murdered in millions in Christian times before the Nazi Holocaust took its six million. Nor are they aware of the almost incessant harassment and degradation visited upon the Jewish people because of their loyalty to their faith. Less again are they aware of the involvment of the Church in this oppression, this capital sin of the Christian past, this "crime of Christendom," as one writer put it. It was the anti-Judaism of Christian theology that formed what Jules Isaac termed the "millenial trunk" from which all other anti-Semitic manifestations thereafter sprang. This historic Christian sin, as yet unacknowledged, remains unrepented.

The legacy of the past has meanwhile taken its toll of the present. The sin of anti-Semitism is not just a sin of our ancestors, but also of their progency, ourselves. But here again it is unacknowledged and unrepented. In my observation anti-Semitism is all but universal among Christians, not of a virulent strain or fully conscious, but low-toned and generally concealed behind disguises of stereotyping, anti-Zionism, Christian zeal, or some other rationalization—and hence almost always denied. It is condemned as a sin in our documents, true; but in reading these condemnations one gains the impression that they speak of a sin of others or of one into which a Christian must not fall, not one of which he or she is, or has ever been, possessed; and there is no reference to the Christian involvement in the past. These things are not said in judgment. Would it be realistic to expect any individual, who is heir to a religious tradition, a centuries-old culture, and born in a secularized world, all of which have been permeated with Judaeophobia, to be free of this animus? A knowledge of history and of self takes on, in this perspective, an unusual significance.

The relevance of anti-Semitism for the Jewish-Christian dialogue, whether as a subject for discussion or personal pathology, has become apparent. If a person is possessed of it to any degree, two things may occur. One is that he or she will eschew the dialogue altogether and thus contribute to the sea of indifference that so often surrounds it. In such a case the lack of awareness of anti-Semitism in history and in self suppresses a most effective source of motivation and all sense of urgency in this area of interfaith relations. Or, alternatively, if he or she does enter the dialogue, he or she will add an ambivalent quality to it, for then every subject discussed will be refracted through the latent bias. It is for reasons like these that this subject is pivotal, indeed the nodal point of the Jewish-Christian dialogue, the point where all other subjects finally intersect. Take any of the major subjects of dialogue: anti-Judaic theology, stereotyping, Jewish-Christian relationships, the Holocaust, the State of Israel, anti-Zionism, the dialogue itself—none of these can be fully explored without encountering anti-Semitism either as a subject or as a condition. This is also why anti-Semitism should ordinarily be taken up first on the agenda. Not a few attempts at dialogue have foundered on the failure to observe this point of sequence.

Let us not take lightly the courage and determination that is required to confront anti-Semitism in a forthright way, be it in dialogue or in social settings. There will invariably be stout, if urbane, resistance to addressing the subject or staying with it for any length of time, and grumblings will be heard about "putting a guilt trip on people," "imputing motives," "seeing anti-Semitism everywhere," and the like. With persistent and graduated exposure to the subject, however, the defensiveness often gives way to a genuine commitment to the struggle against it. Doubtless we are dealing here as much with a conversion of heart as with a gain in knowledge.

A last word on this subject should be said about the imbalance that affects a dialogue in which the Christian party remains impervious to the anti-Semitic problem. Jewish participants are acutely aware of the problem from simple familiarity with the history of the Jewish people and also from having felt its lash in their own lives. Unfortunately, many Jews seem to believe that Christians are quite cognizant of the anti-Semitic situation, and tend as a result to interpret Christian indifference and reluctance with respect to it as insensitivity rather than ignorance. How can a dialogue prosper when one dialogist harbors this unspoken question: *"Why are they so persecution-minded and concentrated on their troubles?"* while this question stands in the mind of the other: *"Why are they so indifferent and callous about the persecution of my people?"*

If the dialogue is to thrive, greater effort must be made to acquaint Christians generally with the burden Jews have borne in history and in their own lives, to convince them of the prevalence of a widespread subliminal Christian anti-Semitism, and to urge them to search their hearts for an animus that is resistant to exposure. Only upon success in these efforts will a major step have been taken to bring to an end this seemingly endless hatred. Only then, I might add, will Christians and Jews be in a position effectively to take a second and more difficult step together: to confront secular anti-Semitism throughout the world, which unquestionably is the most formidable anti-Semitic growth today.

THE HOLOCAUST

Despite its enormity as a happening and as an issue, the Holocaust will not detain us. Among our subjects it has been the most discussed, with the exception of Christian theology. Much has been written about it, but on lower levels of dialogue there exists a reluctance to address it and on the popular level even a resentment towards singling it out from the endless listing of holocausts and genocides that have gained spokespersons in recent years. We have witnessed a concerted effort to deny or diminish the Holocaust, and to rob it of its uniqueness. The motives behind this deserve exploration.

The Holocaust has too often been made by scholars into a purely theological or theodicean problem. Here God becomes the scapegoat, in such wise that the Holocaust is no longer what it really was: the ultimate in anti-Semitism, a summit of human perversity, a monstrous human enterprise long in preparation, which could have been prevented and can, if we so will, be prevented in the future. The Holocaust, theologically, is more a problem of human freedom than one of divine Providence, more a moral than a theological problem.

Finally, there is the problem of Christian responsibility, a sizable subject that we can only touch on here. Rosemary Ruether draws a thin line between Christian and modern racist anti-Semitism, and sees the Holocaust as a stage of Christian anti-Semitism. Actually, Christian and modern racist anti-Semitism are essentially different and in some ways opposites. In a perverted way Christian anti-Semitism was aimed at the salvation of the Jews;

modern racist Jew hatred was ultimately aimed at their extermination. But then, the latter could not have come into existence without the former. Historically, they are continuous. Hitler had to invent nothing new in his assault on the Jews; he had only to add the resources of German science and technology. His Jew was already set up, naked and helpless, awaiting his assault, thanks to a centuries-old process of teaching and oppression that derived primarily from Christian theological anti-Judaism. At the onset and throughout the Holocaust there was the supine posture of the churches. Many heroic Christians spoke out and helped, often with their lives, but it was a minority effort. Here again we face a situation not fully acknowledged and thus again unrepented.

THE STATE OF ISRAEL

If the problem of anti-Semitism lies at the core of Jewish-Christian relations and deserves first place in the agenda of the dialogue, the State of Israel is the ultimate gauge and supreme test of the health and progress of the dialogue. This issue occupies an unrivaled first place among present Jewish concerns, and it is the Jewish choice for first place on the agenda. Fortunately, Jews are less reticent in pressing for this priority than in the case of anti-Semitism. May I say, they can put up with our anti-Semitism, being well used to it, but cannot bear our anti-Zionism. I can understand Jewish worry about anti-Zionism. Anti-Semitism makes Jewish life uncomfortable and today is only occasionally perilous. Jews correctly see anti-Zionism, however, as a thrust against their very existence as a people. Most Christians do not understand this. This time it is not so much a matter of ignorance or a missing page, but a basic Christian misconception of Judaism itself. Many Christians, including Vatican officials, insist on considering Judaism as a religious denomination similar to sectarian institutional affiliations in Christianity. Hence, they are unable to understand its uniqueness as a peoplehood not only in a spiritual sense, but in the sense of a flesh-and-blood historical people formed by a call of God to become a people apart, bonded to the Torah in a Promised Land, the Land of Israel. Failing to see Judaism in this way, as Jews define it according to their own religious experience, Christians denature and dichotomize Judaism, making it solely a religion and Israel solely a matter of politics and real estate.

These are truths that Christians should have known from their experience and from their Scriptures. In any case they were truths soon learned in dialogue. The dialogue was only two years old when it stumbled, I might say, over the State of Israel. It was in 1967, the year of the threat of another genocide against the Jewish people, this time in Israel. It was the year of the Six Day War. Arab armies, equipped by the Soviets, marched on Israel with the expressed intent of "driving every last Israeli into the sea." In their alarm Jews turned to the churches with which they had been in dialogue for a word of support, for a plea for the survival of Israel. It was not forthcoming. Jewish disappointment was great, in some cases bitter, and some Jews ventured the opinion that the Jewish-Christian dialogue was dead. Their mistake was to have expected too much too soon. How could some two thousand years of alienation and hatred be undone in so few years?

What did Israel mean to most Christians in 1967? A small mideastern state—of dubious origin, some would add—in trouble with its neighbors, that was about all. What did it mean to Jews? Almost everything. To learn this we need only go back to 1945. In that year the Jewish people had emerged from the Great War, as everyone else, but they with one-third of their people gone. Intermarriage among Jews had run high before the war and presumably would continue to do so after. In the prognosis of some Jews, intermarriage threatened to give Hitler a posthumous victory: the disappearance of the Jewish people. It was a low moment in Jewish history—a history of many low moments. Then, two years later, quite suddenly, there it was: the State of Israel, an internationally founded Jewish state in the ancient homeland. It was seen as a miracle by many, not all of them Jews. The establishment of the new state fired the hearts of Jews everywhere. It was seized upon as a promise of survival, a new source of self-identity, and, not least, a haven from a ubiquitous and undying anti-Semitism. To the Jew, Israel obviously meant everything.

The dialogue was saved after the 1967 let-down by taking the subject of Israel into the dialogue. Israel's connection with Judaism—in other words, Israel as Jews define it according to their own religious experience—was made clear. In retrospect, it comes as a surprise that so many, even well-educated, Christians found it necessary to learn from Jews of the tie that binds Jews and Judaism to Israel. A simple familiarity with history and with the Hebrew Scriptures would have been sufficient for Christians to arrive at the Jewish position unassisted.

Judaism is essentially Zionist. From its first moments, the Land of Israel, *Eretz Yisrael*, as promised, possessed, or repossessed, has been a constant of Jewish history. The promise appears early in the Bible (Gen. 12:1) and from that point, possession of or return to the Promised Land became a dominant concern in Jewish life. Only on its soil could the Torah be fully implemented; only with Jewish inhabitation of the Land could the Messianic era come about. Throughout the millenia, living in or returning to Zion was a recurring theme of Jewish writings, religious and secular, ancient, medieval, and modern. Jewish liturgy is replete with supplications for return to the Land for rebuilding of Jerusalem. Three times a day throughout the centuries pious Jews prayed in the *Amidah* for that return. Jewish fastdays, the Passover Seder, the Day of Atonement service, Sabbath and holiday prayers gave vent to the yearning of the Jewish soul for their Holy Land. Meanwhile the *Talmud,* that massive corpus of Jewish law and teaching, devotes, I understand, about one-third of its pages to the Land of Israel. The God of Israel, the people of Israel, the Torah of Israel, all, are inextricably linked to *Eretz Yisrael,* the Land of Israel. It is no exaggeration then to say that Judaism is saturated with Zionism. The political movement launched by Theodor Herzl at the turn of the century can be seen, in last analysis, as little more than a latter-day political manifestation of the deep Messianic and Zionist core of Judaism itself. Israel may be seen as a merely political affair by non-Jews, but never so by a committed Jew or a fully knowledgeable and unbiased Christian.

And yet despite this centrality of the Land of Israel in Jewish life and tradition, so often attested by Jewish spokespersons and dialogists, there exists a reluctance to concede it its rightful place on the dialogue agenda, and on the more popular level a mild anti-Zionism persists. By "mild" anti-Zionism, I refer to an opposition that is not of the virulent or rabid kind that one finds in some quarters, but rather simply a tendency, for example, to disfavor Israel, to see Jewish attachment to it as a dual loyalty, to employ a double standard in judging it, to empathize instead with Israel's enemies, to be hypercritical of its actions, or to lack a concern for its peril or survival.

The problem of anti-Zionism should be considered a required discussion for advanced levels of dialogue— preferably introduced by Christian initiative. What are its roots? Does it have an anti-Semitic connection? What influence does the Middle East conflict bring to bear on the problem?

Certainly anti-Zionism and anti-Semitism are not

synonymous. It is possible to be anti-Zionist and not anti-Semitic. But it is also possible to be anti-Zionist *and* anti-Semitic. In my observations, anti-Zionism and anti-Semitism all too often, despite different attire, are difficult to tell apart. One's views on this will depend considerably on how real or prevalent one believes anti-Semitism to be. If it is, as I believe, a close-to-universal, low-toned, latent attribute of Christians (and I might add, of non-Jews generally), it would only be realistic to expect to find it readily in the anti-Zionism of numerous Christians.

The anti-Zionist problem is compounded when we turn to the Middle East conflict, which tends to hang as a cloud over the whole Jewish-Christian encounter, but more especially over the subject of Israel, even when it is confined merely to discussions on the possibility of a Christian theology of Israel. The entire scope of our mutual discussions suffer from a politicization stemming from the conflict. Here I am referring to the refusal, often met with in dialogue, to take up any aspect of the subject of the State of Israel without at the same time considering what is usually referred to as "Arab rights"— as if the racial category "Arab" incudes a religious or theological meaning. This politicizing of the dialogue can only discourage all discussion of Israel in its properly Jewish-Christian context. Rejecting this politicized approach and defending Israel need not, let me emphasize, entail any insensitivity to the rights and aspirations of Palestinian Arabs. Affirmation of the State of Israel or refutation of Arab propaganda must not be equated with a rejection of these rights and aspirations.

And indeed a refutation of current propagandistic myths that cast dark suspicions on the foundations of the State of Israel and on its very right to exist is necessary. It is propaganda that has unfortunately become the conventional view of the situation even among non-Arabs, and has poisoned many minds against Israel and exerted

a damaging effect on discussions of Israel in the dialogue. The propagandizing usually runs like this: an
alien people (the Jews) expelled the indigenous people of
Palestine (the Arabs) from the homeland which they had
occupied from time immemorial, forcing them to fester
in poverty on its borders. This deceptive fiction forms
not only one of the chief sources of Arab enmity to Israel
but also of the cool neutrality, if not hostility, of much of
non-Arab opinion on Israel. It is imperative that this
widespread and calumnious myth be exposed to the light
of true historical evidence if we are to hope for fruitful
discussions on the question of Israel.

Fortunately, recent research has greatly advanced our
understanding of the origins of the conflict. Moreover, it
not only destroys the foregoing myth but largely reverses
it. Records show that many Arabs in Palestine in 1945
were relatively recent arrivals. A large influx of Arabs
occurred in the 1930s and 1940s, the very time when
Jewish immigration was severely restricted and finally
stopped. Many Arabs followed Jewish settlers into the
land in order to partake in their higher standard of
living. When the State of Israel was established by a 33 to
13 vote of the United Nations in 1948, Jews were conceded land only where they constituted a majority.
Meanwhile, after the 1948 war in order to qualify many
Arabs as refugees it was necessary to reduce the standard
international requirement of ten-years' residency to two-
years. Lastly, most Arab refugees who fled from Israel in
1948 were not driven out but left of their own accord,
some encouraged to do so by their own leaders on the
promise that they would be back when Israel was van-
quished by Arab armies.

Unquestionably, the Palestinian people have suffered
in consequence of these developments. It is not a suffering, however, that should be laid at the door of the
Israelis. The Arab leaders, the P.L.O., the United Nations, must accept as much, indeed more, responsibility

for the plight of Palestinians. Israel, moreover, can do little about the situation in advance of a forthright Arab acceptance of Israel's right to exist within secure borders and of face-to-face negotiations by Palestinian leadership with the Israelis.

At all events, it is imperative for the health and progress of the Jewish-Christian dialogue—and indeed for the success of such peace negotiations—that Israel be cleared of the calumnious myths that have overshadowed it as a nation from its first days.

Is it not, meanwhile, the Christian above all who, if for no better reasons than guilt and a sense of reparation, should rejoice in the upturn in the fortunes of the Jews that has been brought about by the return of so many of them to their ancient homeland, which has become for them not only a source of security and a new identity but also for many of us a sign of God's faithfulness to His covenant and promise?

THE BALANCE SHEET

What judgment are we to render finally on the Jewish-Christian performance that has followed upon the issuance of *Nostra Aetate*? Obviously there has been progress, and so we should celebrate. But there has been stasis and even some regress, so we should critique. Celebrate and critique, but in what proportions? Different answers will be given this question according to whether one takes the long- or short-range view. To look at these few years across the millenia that preceded them they are, admittedly, the most satisfying and heartening in all of Jewish-Christian history. But viewed in the short run and in the light of the enormity of the debt we as Christians have inherited from an alienated past and the consequent enormity of the task of reparation and reconstruction that lies ahead, how can we see them but as faltering and slothful? Indeed our pace must quicken. Our dialogue, not an end in itself, must be translated into action. Our consensus in dialogue must be enlarged and consolidated, so that the results of our colloquia will reach their natural habitat: the seminaries, classrooms, pulpits, and, I might also say, the street. The initiative in this comprehensive effort should, for the greatest part, come from Christians, for the debt history bequeaths us is a Christian one. The initiative in the dialogue, despite this, still rests in Jewish hands. Please God, Jews will hold onto it until we overtake them and take over what should have been ours from the start. But then, in the end, it is not primarily in education and dialogue that this godly project belongs but rather in the realm of the spirit, in that *metanoia*, that conversion of heart and mind which every discovery of sins and failings requires.

NOTES

1. This document and others issued by the Vatican and other religious bodies are found in H. Croner, *Stepping Stones to Further Jewish-Christian Relations* (Mahwah, N.J.: Paulist, 1977) and *More Steppingstones to Jewish-Christian Relations* (Mahwah, N.J.: Paulist Press, 1985).
2. *More Steppingstones*, pp. 220–232.
3. For a concise summary of revisionist theology, see J. Pawlikowski, *What Are They Saying about Jewish-Christian Relations?* (Mahwah, N.J.: Paulist, 1980).
4. Principally, Rosemary Radford Ruether, *Faith and Fratricide: The Theological Roots of Antisemitism* (New York: Seabury, 1974).
5. James Hitchcock has succinctly stated this position. See "What Price Harmony?" In *Face to Face: An Interreligious Bulletin*, vol. XI (Spring 1984): pp. 18–19 (Anti-Defamation League, N.Y.).

IV
The Future Agenda

9. A Theology of Religious Pluralism?

JOHN T. PAWLIKOWSKI

> A fully developed and widely accepted theology of religious pluralism remains a challenge still inadequately met by either of our traditions . . . . No one of us can consider ourselves safe from religious attack until this happens.

In assessing the progress we have made since the issue of *Nostra Aetate,* it should be obvious that not everything that needs to be done in theology, religious education, and liturgy has been accomplished. But as Michael Signer points out in his paper, steady, genuine progress has indeed been made, especially in the area of religious education where the major textbook studies of the past decades have exercised a decidedly positive impact. There are too many voices in our midst who are prone to proclaim the death of the dialogue after some euphoric moments just after the end of the council. This tendency appears more frequently in Jewish circles than in Christian ones. Hence a positive attitude toward the last twenty years is most welcome. More interchange is now taking place between Christians and Jews in North America, and increasingly in Europe and South America, than at anytime since our original schism in the first century. The voices of pessimism must not be allowed to obscure the fundamental transformation that is underway in the

Christian understanding of the people of Israel nor the growth that is occurring in our mutual self-understanding.

SIGNER'S MIRRORS AS MODELS FOR JEWISH-CHRISTIAN RELATIONS

As we look to the future, all of us must ponder the models that govern our relationships. Michael Signer has presented an excellent analysis of the model we all employ. I would like to add some reflections of my own in an effort to carry his notions yet another step forward. Signer's contention that a "totally other" model for the Christian-Jewish relationship could prove in the end to be "isolating and self-defeating" opens the door to a discussion that will remain central to our encounter for the foreseeable future. Both practical and theological implications are involved.

On the practical side, any model that emphasizes total distinctiveness may result in Jews and Christians doing nothing more than reacting to *statements* about each other. We shall never discover the secrets of the heart, we shall never know what energizes our respective emotional lives. The 1975 "Guidelines and Suggestions for Jewish-Chritian Relations" urged Catholics to come to understand Jews as *they define themselves*. Ending the Christian practice of relating only to "straw Jews" created by the Christian imagination is a precondition of authentic dialogue. But for this to really happen we Christians must come to know Jews in the totality of their being. We must begin the process of "passing over" into the reality of the Jewish people, as Father John Dunne has termed it, and not confine ourselves merely to the objective examination of Judaism. Signer urges a similar process of Jews vis-à-vis Christianity, and that is all to the good.

How might Jews and Christians accomplish this revision of one another? I believe the "mirror" model, which Signer offers as a replacement for the "totally other" model, to be especially ripe for theology. An enduring link seems implied in the mirror imagery that parallels some of the recent trends in Christian theological reflection on the Church's bond with the Jewish people. In my own work, particularly the volume *Christ in the Light of the Christian-Jewish Dialogue*,[1] I stress that the two covenants must be seen as distinct, but ultimately complimentary. Through dialogue each can resurrect themes latent in their tradition but largely dormant or severely underdeveloped until now. I join with Signer in seeing this "mirror" imagery as very promising for unmasking bonds that we may have imagined never existed. The development of the "universality" motif in pharisaic Judaism is but one example of this.

While I am convinced Signer is moving on the right road, his paper stops short of joining an even more profound discussion now emerging among Christian theologians with a sensitivity to the Church's Jewish context. The question facing these scholars and church leaders is whether we need to move to an affirmation of what some have called a "single covenant" model for explaining the theological link between the two faith communities. The 1985 Vatican "Notes" on Catholic catechesis and Judaism argue against any notion of two parallel lines of salvific liberation for humankind. Jews and Christians rather must be seen as co-partners in the same plan of human redemption. Pope John Paul II, on a number of occasions, has spoken of a special bond between Jews and Christians unlike any the church shares with another world religion. Cardinal Martini of Milan, formerly rector of the Biblicum in Rome, spoke of the break between Church and Synagogue as a "schism" in addressing the 1984 meeting of the International Council of Christians and Jews:

Every schism and division in the history of Christianity entails the deprivation of the body of the Church from contributions which could be very important for its health and vitality, and produces a certain lack of balance in the living equilibrium of the Christian community. If this is true of every great division in Church history, it was especially true of the first great schism which was perpetrated in the first two centuries of Christianity.[2]

This same theological direction can be seen in some recent Protestant statements as well, including a study document prepared by the World Council of Churches.

Many Jews and Christians have applauded this new ecclesial orientation with respect to Judaism. But it has implications that have not been sufficiently probed to date. Does it eliminate all distinctiveness for Judaism? Does it posit a form of reconciliation that might never be acceptable to Jews? How does one incorporate the meaning of the Incarnation into such a model, the one Christian belief that in the eyes of Abraham Joshua Heschel ultimately separates Church from Synagogue? These are questions that remain unanswered by both the Christian proponents of this theological trend and the Jewish religious leaders who have welcomed it. Such a model of intimate bonding carries implications for Jewish self-understanding with respect to Christianity as well as for the Church's theological stance towards Judaism.

In future discussions Jews and Christians must supplement this valuable "mirror imagery" suggested by Signer with a thorough discussion of these contemporary developments in Christian theology. To date, however, the proper balance has not yet been struck. Furthermore, we can realize such a goal only through constructive interchange between Christian and Jewish scholars. Signer seems to favor such a theological encounter, which up till now has been opposed or at least downplayed in most Jewish circles. The time has come for these barriers to fall. We Jews and Christians need to search *together* for a new model that goes beyond the current options of single or double covenants. Both the linkage between Judaism and Christianity and the ongoing distinctiveness of the two covenantal traditions need to be incorporated into any emergent model.

Over and beyond questions of conflict, our encounter with one another can expose us to aspects of religious living that are virtually missing in the practice of our respective faiths. Jews should learn from Christians about retreats, to use Signer's example; Christians might learn to worship in a familial setting. In my judgment pursuit of many such areas of mutual enrichment can move ahead even as we continue to debate which formal theological model best expresses our relationship.

Suffice it to say that Signer's "mirror model" represents one way forward. But to place that image on a sound foundation, we must turn our attention to a constructive theology of religious pluralism.

TOWARD A THEOLOGY OF RELIGIOUS PLURALISM

A fully developed and widely accepted theology of religious pluralism remains a challenge still inadequately met by either of our traditions. Until each of the major world religions goes beyond merely providing religious warrants for toleration or for individual religious liberty and develops a comprehensive statement about the positive values inherent in religious pluralism, we will not be able to close the books once and for all on the history of interreligious strife. No one of us can consider ourselves safe from religious attack until this happens.

Two Israelis, David Hartman and Shemaryahu Talmon, have presented possible options for such a theology from the Jewish perspective. Hartman calls for a deemphasis on absolute truth claims, the primary reason for past interreligious conflict. Instead, we must begin forging a new pluralistic spirituality rooted in a radical, all-embracing abandonment of previous claims to absolute truth which have been common to Judaism, Christianity, and Islam. He rejects any "intermediate" position which views commitment to pluralism as a temporary position by a religious group until it experiences final confirmation of its faith perspective in the eschaton. He writes:

> We cannot in some way leap to some eschaton and live in two dimensions; to be pluralistic now but to be monistic in our eschatological vision is bad faith. We have to recognize that ultimately spiritual monism is a disease.[3]

Shermaryahu Talmon's proposal for a theology of religious pluralism was originally developed for a multilateral dialogue sponsored by the World Council of Churches. As Talmon sees it, several principles are key to such a theology. The first is that it must draw upon the particularistic resources of each faith community. He rejects any approach that would develop its formulation by finding common bases among all religious traditions. Each religion should bring its own distinctiveness to the joint search for such a theology.

Talmon's second principle for a theology of religious pluralism stands in direct opposition to Hartman's viewpoint. Though they may vary as to the degree, most religious traditions harbor dreams of universal acceptance either by force or persuasion. Religious believers, he strongly insists, cannot deny such ultimate aims without being false to their faith-tradition. The crucial question thus arises: How can the various faiths produce a theology of religious pluralism if each really desires universal acknowledgment of its particular spiritual truth? The answer, Talmon suggests, depends on the growth of a common mentality. Having laid their respective eschatological goals on the table, each faith community must agree to look upon the task of building the world community as fundamentally non-eschatological or, at best,

pre-eschatological. This involves the clear resolve that
the process of building global interdependence must
never become the occasion for activist eschatological
realization and for the proselytization that it implies.[4]

Talmon thus clearly differs from Hartman in this perspective. He does not call for the abandonment of eschatological truth claims as a precondition for the development of authentic religious pluralism on a worldwide
scale.

My personal sympathy is far more with Hartman than
with Talmon. There must be some modification of eschatological truth claims for a genuine theology of religious
pluralism. But Talmon too is persuasive: such a theology
cannot be built simply on universal elements in our respective faith traditions, but must grow out of our particularistic dimensions as well. Unlike Talmon, I feel both
dimensions of our traditions—universality and particularity—must come into play. But the question remains a
pivotal one. To what extent can particularity bring us to
an adequate theology of religious pluralism and how is
"adequately" to be determined?

A theology of religious pluralism might allow us to say
we have more than others; but never could it permit us to
say we have a hold on all significant religious insight.
This does not mean that each religious tradition is incap-
able of providing salvation for its adherents. What we
need to recognize is that all of us are saved in our incompleteness. Let me make it clear, however, that all of this
needs further discussion. A theology of religious pluralism is still in its infancy in all of our faith traditions.

In my own work on Christianity's theological relationship to Judaism, developed most fully up till now in
my volume *Christ in the Light of the Christian-Jewish Dialogue* and in an essay on Christology and the Holocaust in
the *Concilium* series,[5] I state some convictions appropriate to the creation of a theology of religious pluralism out
of a Christian context. These are: (1) The "Christ event"
did not invalidate the Jewish faith perspective; (2) Chris-

tianity is not superior to Judaism, nor is it the fulfillment of Judaism as previously maintained; (3) The Sinai covenant is in principle as crucial to Christian faith expression as the covenant in Christ; and (4) Christianity needs to reincorporate dimensions from its original Jewish context.

Behind these convictions stands the realization that a Christology has to be developed which recognizes central and unique features in the revelation of the Christ event without thereby implying that these represent the totality of revelation. Such a Christology needs to make room both for the ongoing validity of the Jewish covenant and for the recognition of its unique and central insights that presently are not incorporated, or at least remain understated, in the Christian churches. This approach to Christology needs to be extended relative to other world religions as well.

Within the context of the Christian-Jewish dialogue, we need to take note of one other aspect of this rethinking of Christology. When we create theological "space" for Judaism (rather than defining Christian identity as totally other) we also moderate, albeit implicitly, any absolutist claims about Christian faith. Because Christianity has so often cast its relationship to Judaism in "over-against" terms, far more than has been the case with the other world religions, any changes in the theological conception of the Christian-Jewish relationship will automatically redound favorably on the Church's ability to relate theologically to these religions as well.

JEWISH-CHRISTIAN RELATIONS AFTER THE HOLOCAUST

Beyond the specific theological models for the Christian-Jewish relationship and the more general framework for a theology of religious pluralism looms a

more basic question: What is the meaning of divine presence in the modern world, especially after the experience of the Holocaust? This question has occasioned a
profound debate in contemporary Judaism that has im-
pacted on Christian thinking as well, especially for such
systematic theologians as David Tracy, Jürgen Molt-
mann, and Johannes Metz.

In previous writings I have called the Holocaust a
central event for theological reflection by both Christians
and Jews.[6] This is certainly the case with respect to its
current implications for the problem of God's justice.
David Tracy has rightly criticized Christian theologians
for virtually ignoring this challenge.[7]

Several Jewish scholars—David Hartman, Eliezer Ber-
kovits, Michael Wyschogrod, and Eugene B. Borowitz
are prominent examples—have downplayed any ultimate theological significance for the *Shoah*. Hartman's
words summarize well the general thrust of this viewpoint:

> Auschwitz, like all Jewish suffering of the past must be
> absorbed and understood within the normative framework
> of Sinai. We will mourn forever because of the memory of
> Auschwitz. We will build a healthy new society because of
> the memory of Sinai.[8]

I stand in partial agreement with these Jewish theologians. Even after the Holocaust our faith expression
must be strongly rooted in the convenantal experiences
and promises. But I believe they have seriously under-
estimated the degree to which the Holocaust forces us to
readjust some of our understanding of our biblical heritages.

Among those Jewish scholars who have argued for
major theological reinterpretation after the Holocaust
the following names stand out: Richard Rubenstein,
Emil Fackenheim, Irving Greenberg, and Arthur
Cohen. Rubenstein has claimed that the Holocaust has

shattered any possible belief in a God of history. The immensity of suffering endured by the supposedly covenanted Jewish people could no longer sustain it. To replace this belief Rubenstein offers contemporary Judaism a new creed of paganism which defines human existence as totally an earthly existence. Greenberg, Fackenheim, and Cohen have not gone as far as Rubenstein in rejecting all previous notions of a convenantal God. But they are unified in their conviction that restatement of the relationship between God and humankind is at the heart of new faith after the Holocaust.

Fackenheim believes that the restoration of the divine image after the experience of the *Shoah* has to acknowledge a certain curtailment of divine power in comparison with past images. A new divine image can only emerge from the testimony to life within the human community, by Holocaust survivors in particular. The desire to bear witness, he says, "turns into a commandment, the commandment to restore the divine 'image' to the limits of his power."[9]

For Irving Greenberg the reality of the Nazi fury forces upon us a thorough reconsideration of the nature of moral obligation for the contemporary Jewish community and seemingly by implication for all those other believers (Christians and Muslims) who in some way regard the Sinai Covenant as fundamental for their faith expression. The end result of any serious reflection on the Sinai Covenant in the face of the divine-human encounter in the Holocaust, as Greenberg sees it, is simply the disappearance of any "commanded" dimension on the part of God.[10]

The third major Jewish figure in the current debate, Arthur Cohen, has undertaken a major reworking of our notion of how God and the human community interact after the Holocaust. Deep reflection on the *Shoah* forces us to recognize, according to Cohen, that we can no longer approach God in a totally traditional fashion.

Gone are the days when we could comfortably picture God as the strategist of human history. The post-Auschwitz God can be legitimately perceived as "the mystery of our futurity, always our *posse,* never acts."[11]

My fundamental sympathies lie basically with the reflections of Fackenheim, Greenberg, and Cohen. God's relationship to the human community cannot be spoken of today as it was pre-*Shoah.* For one, the role of the human community in keeping history free of further eruptions of radical evil akin to Nazism has been strongly enhanced, as all three have correctly insisted. In exercising this new responsibility, humanity will be helping to restore the divine image as Fackenheim has suggested. Humanity finds itself facing the realization that "future" is no longer something God will guarantee. Survival, whether for the people of Israel or humanity at large, is now more than ever a human proposition. In their differing ways Fackenheim, Greenberg, and Cohen have made this fact abundantly clear. And we need to be profoundly grateful for that.

But despite my gratitude I must demur a bit from their approach. The Holocaust has shattered all simplistic notions of a "commanding" God. On this point I go full way with Greenberg, Cohen, and Fackenheim. Such a "commanding" God can no longer be the touchstone of ethical behavior. But the *Shoah* has also expressed humanity's desperate need to restore a relationship with a "compelling" God; *compelling* because we have experienced through symbolic encounter with this God healing, strengthening, and affirming that buries any need to assert our humanity through the destructive, even deadly, use of human power. This sense of a compelling "parent God" who has gifted humanity, whose vulnerability for the Christian has been shown in the Cross, is the meaningful foundation for an adequate moral ethos after the Holocaust. Here I part company to a significant extent with Greenberg, Fackenheim, and Cohen in posit-

ing this "compelling" God. Their approach renders the
divine role too indirect and weak.

Let me now turn to two other issues that must continue
to occupy our attention in the future.

JEWISH-CHRISTIAN WORSHIP

The first is the question of worship. This is partly a
joint problem, and partly an exclusively Christian concern. Both Jews and Christians have to face up to the
question, what is meaningful worship after the Holocaust? And if we take the emerging theological model of
partnership as seriously as we should, then we shall have
to reflect on how our liturgical celebrations can under-
gird this image.

On the Christian side, there are some special problems, which include the following: (1) the reading, often
quite dramatized, of the Passion Narratives in the Holy
Week liturgies; (2) the handling of the prophetic readings in Advent and Lent; (3) how the Psalms fit into
worship; (4) preaching from the Hebrew Scriptures and
the lectionary's selection of texts from them; (5) the por-
trayal of the link between the Holy Thursday liturgy and
Passover; (6) creating a tone in the Christian liturgy
which clearly shows the continuity of the Jewish covenant
in line with emerging Christian theology; (7) developing
liturgies that would pick up on the Jewish celebration of
creation; (8) creating liturgies that would move away
from excessive reliance on a Christology emphasizing the
fulfillment of messianic prophecies; and (9) possible
Christian celebration of certain Jewish festivals.

The area of liturgy remains much less reformed in
light of the Christian-Jewish dialogue since *Nostra Aetate*
than either religious education or theology. It needs our
immediate attention. For it still generally harbors a "fulfillment" (and by implication "displacement") approach
to the theology of the Christian-Jewish relationship.

AN INTERRELIGIOUS COALITION: PEACE
WITH JUSTICE

Finally, we shall have to turn our attention anew to the area of peace with justice. We need to rebuild the inter-religious coalition we once had on civil rights. Our focus now must be on both the domestic and international scenes in the age of global interdependence. I believe we may be starting again. Jewish contributions to the Catholic bishops' Economics Pastoral have been significant. The Catholic Bishops' Conference and the Union of American Hebrew Congregations have issued a joint study guide on the Peace Pastoral which provides us with a model for reasoned debate not only on peace but on such highly controversial issues as abortion. Such a spirit of reasoned debate must be returned to the public sphere in the United States. We Christians must also recognize that if we take seriously the new theological view of a partnership with Judaism in the redemption of human-kind we must take into account both classical and modern Jewish perspectives on key social issues.

But in addition to more practical concerns, we will need to focus on underlying theological issues that shape our reponses to concrete social questions. Here I am thinking of the issue of power. Many Jewish commenta-tors on the Holocaust, such as Richard Rubenstein and Irving Greenberg, insist that one critical lesson of the Holocaust is that all peoples need to acquire an adequate measure of power to survive. Irving Greenberg has called its assumption inescapable after the *Shoah*. Such assumption of power must be coupled with the creation of better mechanisms of self-criticism, correction, and repentance. To reject power would render us slaves of bloodshed and an exploitative status quo.

The Catholic bishops' Peace Pastoral will no doubt intensify the discussion of power in the dialogue. This is a positive development, though it could be marked by some tension given the present conflicts in the Middle

East. Christians, in developing a theology of peace, must seriously wrestle with the reflections on power resulting from meditations on the post-*Shoah* meaning of the God-human community relationship. This is required by the new theological sense of a profound covenantal linkage between our two faith communities. On the other hand, Jews, who have not had the experience of power for very long, can hopefully profit from the ongoing reflections on power and its abuse which the bishops' pastoral has so sensitively placed before us.

As one who has studied the Holocaust extensively, I feel that the reflections on power by Greenberg and his colleagues are crucially important for a discussion of peace in our time. The total rejection of power and active resistance as a component of the quest for justice could easily result in greater injustice. But willingness to assume power in a nuclear age clearly demands the estab-lishment of definite norms for its use and the abrogation of some of its forms and concentrations.

As we look back upon *Nostra Aetate*, let us celebrate the growth of our new mutuality. Problems and tensions will remain. But the prospects for increased strength to face them and an enriched understanding of the meaning of God's sustaining presence in this post-*Shoah* age are in-deed bright as a result of our deepening engagement both in mind and heart. Let us always recall the clear message of our common teachers, the biblical prophets: What ultimately matters is the quality of life we lived together along the way towards that final reign of God we all eagerly await.

NOTES

1. John T. Pawlikowski, *Christ in the Light of the Chris-tian-Jewish Dialogue* (Mahwah, N.J.: Paulist Press, 1982).

2. Cardinal Martini, in the *Martin Buber House,* September (1984): p. 9.

3. David Hartman, in *Immanuel,* Spring (1976): p. 79.

4. Shemaryahu Talmon, in the *Ecumenical Review,* October (1974): p. 617.

5. John T. Pawlikowski, "Christology and the Holocaust," in Elizabeth Schüssler-Fiorenza and David Tracy, eds., *The Holocaust as Interruption* (Edinburgh: T&T Clark, 1984).

6. See for example, John T. Pawlikowski, *The Challenge of the Holocaust for Christian Theology* (New York: Anti-Defamation League of B'nai B'rith, 1982).

7. See David Tracy, in Abraham J. Peck, ed., *Jews and Christians after the Holocaust* (Philadelphia: Fortress Press, 1982), p. 101.

8. David Hartman, in the *Ecumenist,* November/December (1982): p. 8.

9. Emil Fackenheim, *The Jewish Return into History* (New York: Schocken, 1978), p. 251.

10. Irving Greenberg, *The Voluntary Covenant* (National Jewish Resource Center, 1982), p. 15.

11. Arthur A. Cohen, *The Tremendum* (New York: Crossroad, 1981), p. 97.

10. *Nostra Aetate*: Between 70 and 1970

DAVID B. BURRELL

> We Americans might cease posing the issue in *our* terms of *Church* and *State*, and consider that history is better represented with three variables: *People* (or nation), *Faith* (or religion), and *State*.

In 1979, Karl Rahner boldly recast the history of Christianity, in a lecture entitled "Toward a Fundamental Theological Interpretation of Vatican II."[1] Rahner focused his attention on those crises that provoked a shift in the theological center of gravity, and so located 70 and 1970 C.E. as symbolic dates: the destruction of the Temple in Jerusalm presaged the "parting of the ways" by precipitating the need to discriminate Jewish believers in Jesus from the rest of the nation, and the aftermath of Vatican II (together with the events in world history) signalled the end of what came into being in 70, namely, western European Christianity. As a result of Rahner's thought, the opening of Christianity to a world of "other religions" must be seen to depend in large part on our capacity as Christians to understand what happened when Jews and Christians parted company. Clearly, Rahner demands a more tensive formulation of the relation-*cum*-differences than those metaphors invoked by many of the Church Fathers and canonized during the Reformation. Moreover, the point of Rahner's linking 1970 with 70 is to remind Christians that we will continue to misconstrue other religions so long as we persist in caricaturing our own roots in Judaism—a people and a way that cannot be circumscribed as a mere religion.

My experience in Israel of the *Shabbat* and of rabbinic thought processes helped me to overcome some initial misperceptions rooted in New Testament polemics against the Pharisees and the Sabbath. More positively, I came to appreciate, largely through celebrating the *Shabbat,* just how creation itself is God's primary gift or grace, as well as the need of any faith tradition to identify itself in terms of law, land, and people. On a more specifically theological note, I came to realize that the issues which emerged in the "parting of the ways" remain formative for Christians' understanding of themselves, and to release the tension between the convenants (for Jew or for Christian) is to tempt each tradition to a specific "triumphalism." If one can still speak (albeit mostly residually) of "unrepentant, unrenewed Christian bodies linked to the strength of empires," that stricture takes on a new and transferred meaning for Jews today in the light of the *Realpolitik* of the State of Israel.

Rahner's proposal to link Christians' appreciation of other world religions with the unique place of a "Christian theology of Judaism" (to use Paul van Buren's felicitous phrase) matches the political facts of *Nostra Aetate* in the context of Vatican II. If the key to passing the statement on the Church and the Jews turned on including that statement in an interfaith, intercultural perspective, it may be that the key to understanding the realities broached by the statement also lies in pursuing them in a more inclusive manner. Allow me to locate two current obstacles to such understanding, one from the Christian, and the other from the Jewish side. By 'obstacles' I mean attitudes which keep both sides from perceiving just how central to their respective self-understandings is the concerted effort to understand the other. And so long as we fail to perceive that, the Jewish-Christian question reduces to Jewish-Christian relations, and remains marginal to each community's efforts to educate its own people in their faith.

Speaking first as a Christian, one must acknowledge that the specific effort which Paul van Buren calls "the Christian theology of Judaism" will be the work of a few. But the more basic fact remains: in the measure that the Church fails to draw sustenance from the root it shares with Judaism, it is that much less than it is called to become. The shared sense of creation as God's primal gift, a sacramental sense of space and time, and the very capacity to hear the prophetic words of Jesus, are all at stake. And while we have made some progress in excising explicitly anti-Jewish portions from catechetical materials, we have made practically none in integrating those perspectives into our theological instruction—at collegiate or seminary or even graduate levels. Because, with a few notable exceptions, graduate schools proceed theologically, quite oblivious to how they might translate Karl Rahner's challenge into their curriculum. Philosophers of religion, on the other hand, tilt away at their perennial foil—the unbeliever—quite unaware that "other believers" could prove an even more interesting interlocutor, and certainly present themselves more readily in the larger world of today. What this means in fact is that Christian students, even and perhaps especially at those institutions where some effort is being made to introduce them to their scriptural heritage, are being introduced to that heritage in a fashion which may not effectively challenge their ingrained presumptions that the testaments, old and new, stand opposed to each other as do justice and love.

A quite laudable attention to Christian origins more often does not reach behind the ready ways of releasing the tension formulated in the period of Christian dominance (those nineteen centuries bracketed by Rahner) to pick up a sense of the struggle that gripped Paul. And in the measure that those stereotyped ways of releasing the tension ("spirit/matter," "reality/shadow") left Jews no theological place to stand, we must acknowledge our complicity in preparing the scene for persecutions and for the still-recent genocide of Auschwitz. The "supercession" or "replacement" schemes do not leave us with actual blood on our hands, to be sure, but they offer a ready rationalization for those intent on eradicating differences by making Jews a theological anachronism. Correlatively, a simple recognition that those formulae also conspire to offer us Christians an easy escape from facing our destiny could set us on a new path. (John Wilkinson puts it masterfully in his *Jerusalem as Jesus Knew It,* "Past attempts by Christians to interpret the Passion in such a way as to condemn modern Jews exemplify the very attitudes the Passion-Narratives were designed to challenge.")[2] But accepting that challenge and blazing that path requires imaginative work by normally unadventuresome academics. On the positive side, however, some individuals and even some institutions are retooling to meet the demand.

On the Jewish side, one cannot help but observe how the State of Israel and its position in the Middle East conflict tends so totally to absorb contemporary Jewish discussion as to place larger issues of self-understanding at risk, to say nothing of Jewish self-understanding in relation to Christianity. I say this acutely aware of the need for an Israel, and of the inescapable fact that there cannot be such a nation without its also being a state. Yet I have also been made aware that putting on a state involves quite a bit more than slipping on a T-shirt for a morning run: there is a logic and there are consequences to statehood which cannot be removed at will or by wishing a "Jewish State" to be something of another order. This realization can be illustrated by an interview with Gershom Scholem (during the spring of 1980 in the *New York Review*) and by an article of Nahum Goldman published in the same journal just after his death in the summer of 1981.

Gershom Scholem noted how the early settlers of the Land of Israel, with their preoccupations for founding a new *society*, were themselves more willing than not to bracket the issue of statehood, often presuming that some accommodation would have to be made with the people of the land when the Palestine mandate had run its course. What changed all that was less ideology (though many Zionists always aspired to a Jewish state) than it was the brutal fact of postwar emigration to Palestine of countless people in search not so much of a vision as of a refuge from terror. Given the new configuration in the Land, and the realities of international life, the option for statehood became an inevitability. Nahum Goldman's observations underscored certain consequences of that decision, in contrasting the situation of Jews in Diaspora with Israelis in more recent times. The shoe is more and more on the other foot, as Diaspora Jews become susceptible to being held hostage by actual policies of the State of Israel, perhaps literally so, but what is more significant, morally. This can be illustrated poignantly in the United States, where a community known to be in the forefront of the battle for civil and legal rights of minorities finds itself expected to support a *de facto* situation of dominance over more than a million people living within the effective boundaries of the State of Israel, yet denied any voice in that state and "enjoying" a clearly diminished standard of justice. That situation— intolerable for Arabs and for Jews—can be addressed fruitfully from the two statements on Israel in the recent

Vatican "Notes on the Correct Way to Present Jews and Judaism in Preaching and Catechesis in the Roman Catholic Church."

The first statement: *"Christians are invited to understand this religious attachment [to the land] which finds its roots in biblical tradition, without, however, making their own any particular religious interpretation of this relationship"* (para. 25): Most Jews I know would welcome such a statement when it comes to the "particular religious interpretations" they must counter within the Jewish scene; but the reference here to the United States bishops' declaration of 1975 points not to the extreme right-wing claims of "religious" Jews, but to those staked out by "dispensational" evangelicals.

The "Notes'" theological admonition is balanced by a second statement, informed by Catholic social teaching. *"The existence of the state of Israel and its political options should be envisaged not in a perspective which is in itself religious, but in their reference to the common principles of international law"* (Ibid.): Again, while many of my Israeli friends would welcome such an admonition from the establishment rabbis in Israel, these directions are addressed to Christians (and specifically to Catholics), as if to say: do not let a "religious interpretation" overshadow or push aside relevant ethical considerations as they attend statecraft. Let *Realpolitik* be called by its proper name, and do not let yourselves be bullied (or cajoled) into offering anything other than a qualified assessment of the actions of *any* state. The American bishops, from a perspective far more international than that of the White House, have been urging a similar course of reflection and action on American Catholics with regard to issues of war and peace and of economic justice. What I am suggesting is that the Jewish community needs a similar voice.

Allow me to suggest a final image as a way to gain a fresh purchase on the current situation. It stems from a

Spanish author writing in the context of the civil war: José Gironella. His novel *The Cypresses Believe in God* presumes the stereotyped face-offs which bedeviled that conflict: Catholics were expected to endorse the *status quo,* and advocates of social justice had to be Marxist. The novel succeeds as well as it does by depicting a young believer passionate for social justice. (It is worth recalling that Catholicism of the 1930s knew but the faintest echoes of anything like a "theology of liberation.") Similarly, in Israel today, whoever favors Arab rights is presumed to be a "secular Jew," and anyone in the "religious" camp is deemed to be an ultra-nationalist. As a result, one of the most interesting groups currently active in Israel is the religious movement for peace, *Oz veShalom.* And as a way to give such groups more room, we Americans might cease posing the issue in our terms of *Church* and *State,* and consider that history is better represented with three variables: *People* (or nation), *Faith* (or religion), and *State.* This combination allows one to characterize, for example, the nineteenth-century nation-state, leaving religious groups outside the combination as potential agents for change; Diaspora Judaism as a people of faith, with the state outside as an independent actor (and, often enough, a threat), Christendom as a union of faith with state, allowing ethnic groupings to pose some difficult questions to that power complex. In such terms, the neatest situation—one which combines all three—can also be suspected as the least open to challenge and change. One thinks of "dear old England" or Lutheran Prussia or what some religious Israelis would make of Israel.

These images, taken together with the suggested reading of the recent Vatican "Notes" can offer a fresh approach for Jews and Christians in approaching the question of Israel and Judaism today. Moreover, like the questions posed to Christian theology by Karl Rahner, they are not peripheral but central to the self-understanding of a people of faith today.

NOTES

1. Karl Rahner, "Toward a Fundamental Theological Interpretation of Vatican II," *Theological Studies* 40: pp. 716–727.

2. John Donald Wilkinson, *Jerusalem as Jesus Knew It. Archeology as Evidence* (London: Thames and Hudson, 1978), p. 44.

11. The Very Depths of Our Pain

ABRAHAM J. PECK

> "Rabbi, you are my master, my guide; I love you, I love you." Whereupon the Rabbi looked sadly at the student and shook his head: "My son, how can you love me, until you know what hurts me?"

The many symposia organized in celebration of the twentieth anniversary of *Nostra Aetate* have been and promise to remain an extraordinarily rich blend of experience and thought. They reflect the genuine quest of a substantial group of Catholics and Jews, men and women, for greater mutual understanding as well as an appreciation of the creative differences that must continue if we are to go forward in our respective faith communities. They assess an event and its consequences that for Jews and Judaism throughout the world has had a historic and truly momentous meaning.

The Declaration *Nostra Aetate*, adopted in October 1965 by the Second Vatican Council, was, as a statement by the French bishops made very clear, "a turning point in the Christian attitude toward Judaism, a breakthrough in attitudes for the future." We have much of that future before us and it remains unknown, but the two decades since *Nostra Aetate* have given Jews a new hope for their children's future, one free from the painful and tragic road travelled by Christians and Jews for nearly two thousand years.

A PAINFUL, TRAGIC ROAD

Yet that road has not always been entirely a straight one. In a century such as this one of unparalleled mass murder of Jews, a few divergences from that path have taken place.

Perhaps the most memorable of these, a dialogue between a liberal Protestant theologian, Karl Ludwig Schmidt, and the great Jewish theologian, Martin Buber, was held in Stuttgart on January 18, 1933, just two weeks before the Nazi seizure of power. I believe this was an important breakthrough in the Jewish-Christian encounter and pointed to the potential for meaningful interfaith discussion despite Schmidt's final words of rebuttal:

> As I have already pointed out, the New Testament recurrently emphasizes that this proclamation, this action of the part of God, is not preliminary but final, once and for all. Nonetheless, we Christians, like the Jews, look to the end. But we dare to do so only by virtue of the fact that God in Jesus Christ has already caused the end to be at hand. We now are wont to speak of the coming of Jesus Christ at the end of time as his Second Coming, his return. For the communion (*Gemeinschaft*) of the Christians with Jews is only preliminary. Were the Church more Christian than it is, the conflict (*Auseinandersetzung*) with Judaism would be sharper than it can now be. From the very beginning of Christianity, this sharp conflict has existed . . . . We Christians must never tire of keeping this one conflict alive.[1]

These words, I believe, were indicative of the course followed by Christianity for the better part of two millennia. Such a course was essentially Marcionite in its solution to the question of whether Christianity or Judaism stood as the proper heir to the promise of Israel. It was Marcion, an early Christian theologian, who suggested that Christianity entirely purge itself of its Jewish roots by excluding the Jewish Bible from its canon of Scripture and by viewing the God of Israel as detrimental to the growth of Christianity. Marcion's arguments were branded heretical, but in rescuing the God of Israel and the Jewish Bible, other Christian thinkers deflected Marcion's attack on the God of the Jews onto the Jewish people.[2]

That was anti-Semitism at the Church's beginnings. And it changed only in form, hardly in degree. When the Christian Imperium gave way to the nation-state, the Jew remained the great "nay-sayer"—first to the acceptance of Jesus as Savior and then to the integral qualities which made one a German, or a Pole, or an Englishman. Yet this last "no" was a qualified one, and was ultimately imposed on the Jew by racist thinkers who decided his "alien" status through their pseudo-scientific analyses of the "Jewish character."

And so it stood until the middle of the twentieth century. Judaism had a negative function and witness, blind to the truth of Christianity's triumph.

It was only when the teachings of Marcion were implemented by the Nazi churches, the *Deutsche Christen* [the "German Christians"] and the *Deutsche Volkskirche* [the "German people's Church"], and not only Judaism but Jewish lives were purged from the midst of Christianity, that the need to change all of this became acute, became necessary to save Christianity itself.[3]

The change began as early as 1943 when the World Council of Churches, then still in formation, submitted a formal memorandum, in conjunction with the World Jewish Congress, to the governments of Britain and the

United States, stating that it had proof of the Nazi "Final Solution" and suggesting rescue efforts. This marked the first time in history that a worldwide body of Christians officially stood up for the Jewish people.[4]

FRENCH JEW, ITALIAN POPE

But how can we forget the role of Jules Isaac, that quiet, unassuming French Jewish survivor of the Holocaust? Here was a man whose entire family, with the exception of a son, perished at the hands of the Nazis. Jules Isaac did not fall into a dark night of despair or cut himself off from a world which had stood by while such horrors were committed in the name of God. No, he brought the implications of the centuries-old Christian attitude towards Judaism before the world. It was Jules Isaac who traced the roots of anti-Semitism to a distinctive set of unfounded theological myths which he termed the "teaching of contempt." It was Jules Isaac who showed the world that Hitler's war against the Jews had been preceded by a much older war of the Church against Judaism. Through Isaac's relentless efforts to convince the Church of its disastrous course of theological development at the Oxford and Seeligsberg conferences in the mid-1940s, a new awareness did take place.

In 1960, Jules Isaac was granted a private audience with Pope John XXIII, the greatest Pope of this or perhaps any other century. As a result of their "lengthy, earnest, and friendly conversation,"[5] history was made. For the first time in nearly twenty centuries the Church actually heard the pleas of a Jew.

Nostra Aetate, which Jules Isaac did not live to see, was a direct result of this historic meeting between the French Jew and the Italian Pope.

THE DEPTHS OF OUR PAIN

We Jews clearly understand that neither *Nostra Aetate* nor the "Guidelines" for its implementation, adopted a decade later in 1975, was a document addressed specifically to us.[6] Rather, we understand that these efforts on the part of the Church were a sincere examination of the Christian conscience in a rather extraordinary manner.

Professor Alfred Gottschalk, the president of the Hebrew Union College-Jewish Institute of Religion, is fond of telling the following Hasidic tale. It deals with a young student who came to a rabbi and disclosed: "Rabbi, you are my master, my guide; I love you, I love you." Whereupon the rabbi looked sadly at the student and shook his head: "My son, how can you love me, until you know what hurts me?"

Nostra Aetate and the "Guidelines" have shown Jews that Christians are beginning to understand what hurts us. Christians now understand that Judaism is not a fossilized, extinct religion, but a legitimate living expression of Jewish belief and has been so in the entire period since the birth of Christianity.

There are at least two distinct aspects of progress in Jewish-Christian relations which highlight the decades since *Nostra Aetate*.

THE TEACHING OF CONTEMPT

The first aspect has been the sincere effort on the part of the major Christian churches, but especially the Catholic church, to purge and repudiate the "teaching of contempt." Father Edward Flannery wrote nearly a decade ago that "the crime of anti-Semitism is an integral part of Christian history (and) will probably transform the Christian mind in a revolutionary way."[7] Father Flannery has understood our anguish as Jews, our hurt, and explained it in a brilliant manner.[8] But I wonder, as he points out, just how far this has been perceived by the greater Christian world.

There is, as Flannery mentioned, a small but important group of Christians in America and abroad who believe that Christianity—in order to become authentic—must experience a radical *metanoia* of the mind [a turning around, a *teshuva*] in the manner in which it views Jews and Judaism as well as the manner in which Christianity understands itself.

Yet, I disagree with the most radical of these theologians, both Catholic and Protestant, whose vision of *metanoia* is such that it paves the way for a theological reconciliation between Judaism and Christianity by tying both religions in a fraternal bond. I believe Jews must question whether this is what we need or expect. As Professors Thomas A. Idinopulos and Roy Bowen Ward point out, "The history of Judaism shows that Jews felt little or no reason to change the original Rabbinic assessment of Christianity as a messianic sect. One should not doubt that deep theological differences exist and are sharply felt."[9] While it is important to ground Christianity in its Jewish antecedents, a common theology is not the logical or necessary outcome of such an effort. I would much rather see, on the part of both Catholic and Protestant theologians, the intensification of what Catholic theologian David Tracy has called a "hermeneutics of suspicion, based on a recognition of ambiguities in the tradition alongside (not replacing) a hermeneutics of retrieval based on a fundamental trust in the tradition."[10] Otherwise the most radical efforts to reshape Christian theology stand to denude Judaism of its religious self-identity and threaten to pursue a policy of spiritual relativism where Christians and Jews could view their religions interchangeably.

JEWISH-CHRISTIAN DIALOGUE

Definable progress has also been made in a second area, namely in the Jewish-Christian dialogue. I use the term "progress" guardedly. The Jewish folk memory has never forgotten the spectacle of the disputations of the Middle Ages. Christian theologians would force Jewish ones to discuss concepts such as "the Messiah" and "the Chosen People." The prearranged outcome of these disputations led to the Jewish side being banished or compelled to witness the burning of the Talmud as the price for participation. To underscore the serious obstacle of these events, Professor Jakob J. Petuchowski has observed that "there will be no possibility of ever really improving relationships until both Christians and Jews have come to terms with their medieval past."[11]

We have, as one Rabbi has written, gone "beyond tea and sympathy" in the interfaith dialogue. But we, together with my colleague, must ponder the question of just *how* far.[12] In the period immediately after *Nostra Aetate* the distinguished Jewish theologian, Rabbi Abraham Joshua Heschel, fearful of the long history of conversionary orientation inherent in the Jewish-Christian dialogue, suggested that certain questions dealing with theology, doctrine, and religious ideology be avoided.[13] That suggestion certainly fit an America whose strong sense of pragmatism and "slapping-on-the-back fellowship" is more the norm than the exception. There is a certain truth to the statement by the social philosopher, Arthur A. Cohen, who referred to the "myth of the Judeo-Christian tradition" in American life: a myth built, he argues, "on a shallow rhetoric in which distinctions are fudged, diversities reconciled, differences overwhelmed by sloppy and sentimental approaches to falling in love after centuries of misunderstanding and estrangements."[14]

Thus it is sobering to learn from a recent sociological

study that efforts of Roman Catholic officials to lift the charge of deicide from the hands of the Jewish people have had little success with large numbers of Catholics. Yet one must understand that to conform to this American conception of interfaith relations, United States Catholic guidelines have necessarily been "pragmatic and non-theological."[15]

A critical area of tension within the dialogue, perhaps less perceptible than it should be, is the presence of a clear-cut asymmetry. Christians are impelled by theology, by the mystery of the Jewish rejection of Christianity, while Jews are interested in facts, in history, in discussing the series of Christian attitudes toward the Jews, attitudes which affected their humanity and produced martyrdom and suffering.[16]

Jews and Christians are engaged in a dialogue that seems to be effective, but I believe their agendas remain far apart. No clearer example of this can be shown than the document issued by the Vatican in June of 1985 entitled "Notes on the Correct Way to Present Jews and Judaism in Preaching and Catechesis in the Roman Catholic Church." This document, several years in the making by Vatican-appointed consultants, is a follow-up of the *Nostra Aetate* declaration and the "Guidelines." While it includes several important positive statements, the most recent document is disappointing in at least two areas—the Holocaust and the State of Israel. Apparently Christians may know what hurts us, but they still do not understand the depths of our pain.

THE HOLOCAUST

As for the Holocaust, Jews now understand that it turned the one obsessive factor that united Christendom for centuries, namely the "Jewish question," into a "Christian question." Rev. Robert A. Everett, whose dissertation on James Parkes,[17] of blessed memory, deserves publication, is correct when he writes that the questions posed by the Holocaust for Jews are fundamentally different from those posed for Christians. Jews ask: "How do we survive in a world that watched silently while we were being killed? And what do we teach our children about this world?"[18] Today, Jews feel each tortuous death, each frightening deportation, each nameless resting place of our brothers and sisters and our children, so many children.

Christians as well as Jews are faced today with the recognition that the Holocaust made a mockery of all our moral values, of our belief in progress, of religious tolerance and understanding. We must understand that these two events, the Holocaust and nuclear destruction—one real and the other the push of a button away—are but two sides of the same phenomenon. One marked the end of Western civilization's innocence; the other will mark the end of our world.

And you must explain to me how we can speak about an authentic Christianity or an authentic Christian until Christians understand that the Holocaust was a "Christian" catastrophe, and how in its wake, the killers and the bystanders could still call themselves Christians.

It is with a sense of civic pride in Cincinnati that I can point to the historian David Wyman's report in his magnificent book *The Abandonment of the Jews* about the declaration of one hundred Cincinnati ministers who stated in August of 1942, when the first reports of the Nazi plan for the extermination of European Jews began to emerge: "We of the Christian ministry cannot and will not remain silent before the spectacle of mass murder suffered by Jews of Nazi-controlled Europe." The Cincinnati ministers pointed out something that, according to Wyman, "should have been obvious, but which seem[s] to have gone unrecognized in American Christian circles during World War II."[19] I spoke with David Wyman recently and he expressed his regret that even today most Christians do not realize that the Holocaust was every bit as much a Christian tragedy as a Jewish one.

This same feeling has been expressed by Father Edward Flannery. Jews have bought his classic work, *The Anguish of the Jews.* Christians have not. And how ironic that 1985 marks the twentieth anniversary not only of *Nostra Aetate,* but also of this volume's publication. Perhaps it too deserves symposia and reappraisal. At least we have the satisfaction of knowing that a revised version of the book has been published by the Paulist Press in 1985.

THE STATE OF ISRAEL

Now we must address the question of Israel. Christians may understand its political meaning for Jews and even its theological meaning for us. But they must also understand the human dimension of its meaning. Without it, every Jew outside of the State becomes part of the "ghost nation" of Jews who are hostage to every oppressor and have no homeland to which to turn.

Without Israel, we remain the "wandering Jew," eternally powerless, condemned to wander for our supposed sins.

These are formidable obstacles in our relationship and I have mentioned them in the true sense and spirit of dialogue. But I will not speak only of our *Leidensgeschichte,* our Jewish history of suffering, or of the Christian sense of a history full of oppressive acts and full of guilt.

Christians have touched the very soul of the Jewish people in the past twenty years. Jews admire Christian introspection and anguish. We look forward to the mutual investigation by Jews and Christians of what the great Jewish theologian Franz Rosenzweig called "the bond of community and non-community," that which has united and that which has separated both faith communities throughout time.

This special moment of reflection on *Nostra Aetate* must not be allowed to fade into the memory of other stillborn revolts. This breakthrough in the relationship between Catholic and Jew must achieve a mutual knowledge and respect between Jews and Christians, the deepening of faith for both our traditions, and an increased mutual concern for our world now and tomorrow.

We have both come a long way from the deep dark night of hatred which has been our legacy. The light of God's Kingdom awaits us all—Jews and Christians, men and women, young and old, black and white, free and oppressed. Today and from now on let us join hands and hearts to walk together until that light is truly ours.

NOTES

1. Quoted in Paul R. Mendes-Flohr, "Ambivalent Dialogue. Jewish-Christian Theological Encounter in the Weimar Period," in *Judaism and Christianity under the Impact of National Socialism* (1919–1945) International Symposium on Judaism and Christianity under the Impact of National Socialism, 1919–1945 (Tel Aviv: Historical Society of Israel, 1982).

2. On Marcion's thought see, among other works, John G. Gager, *The Origins of Anti-Semitism: Attitudes toward Judaism in Pagan and Christian Antiquity* (New York: Oxford University Press, 1983), pp. 162ff.

3. Ekkehard Hieronimus, "Zur Religiosistät der völkischen Bewegung" and Hubert Cancik, "Neuheiden und totaler Staat. Völkische Religion am Ende der Weimarer Republik," both in *Religions und Geistesgeschichte der Weimarer Republik*, Hubert Cancik, ed. (Duesseldorf: Patmos, 1982).

4. Gerhart Riegner, *A Warning to the World* (Cincinnati, Ohio: Hebrew Union College-Jewish Institite of Religion, 1983), p. 15.

5. Glaire Huchet Bishop, "Jules Isaac: A Biographical Introduction," in Jules Isaac, *The Teaching of Contempt* (New York: Holt, Rinehart, and Winston, 1964), p. 13.

6. Henry Siegman, "A Decade of Catholic-Jewish Relations—A Reassessment" in Richard W. Rousseau, ed., *Christianity and Judaism: The Deepening Dialogue* (Scranton, Pa.: Ridge Row Press, 1983), p. 160.

7. Edward H. Flannery, "Response to Henry Siegman," in Rousseau, *Christianity and Judaism*, p. 174.

8. Edward H. Flannery, *The Anguish of the Jews. Twenty-Three Centuries of Anti-Semitism* (New York: Macmillan, 1965).

9. Thomas A. Idinopulos and Roy Bowen Ward, "Is Christology Inherently Anti-Semitic? A Critical Review of Rosemary Reuther's *Faith and Fratricide*" in *Journal of the American Academy of Religion* 45/2 (1977): p. 208.

10. David Tracy, "Religious Values After the Holocaust: A Catholic View," in Abraham J. Peck, ed., *Jews and Christians After the Holocaust* (Philadelphia: Fortress Press, 1982), p. 88.

11. Jakob J. Petuchowski, "Christian-Jewish Dialogue," in *The Jewish Spectator* (Winter 1982), p. 23.

12. Leon Klenicki, "From Fellowship, Tea, and Sympathy to a Change of Heart: The Interreligious Dialogue in the United States," in *Ecumenism* (December 1): p. 21.

13. S. Daniel Breslauer, "Theological Issues and Christian-Jewish Dialogue," in *Religion: Journal of the Kansas School of Religion* 1: p. 1.

14. Arthur A. Cohen, *The Myth of the Judeo-Christian Tradition* (New York: Harper and Row, 1969), p. 217.

15. Idinopulos and Ward, "Is Christology Inherently Anti-Semitic," 195; Charlotte Klein, "Catholics and Jews—10 Years After," *Journal of Ecumenical Studies* 4 (Fall 1975): p. 477.

16. This point is emphasized by Michael Cook, "Envisioning a New Symmetry in Jewish-Christian Dialogue," in Jakob J. Petuchowski, ed. *Defining a Discipline. The Aims and Objections of Judeo-Christian Studies* (Cincinnati, Ohio: Hebrew Union College-Jewish Institute of Religion, 1984).

17. Robert A. Everett, "James Parkes: Historian and Theologian of Jewish-Christian Relations," Ph.D. diss. Columbia University, 1983.

18. Robert A. Everett, "The Impact of the Holocaust on Christian Theology," in *Christian-Jewish Relations* (December 1982): p. 6.

19. David Wyman, *The Abandonment of the Jews: America and the Holocaust, 1941–1945* (New York: Pantheon Books, 1984), p. 26.

12. *Nostra Aetate* and the New Jewish-Christian Feminist Dialogue

DEBORAH McCAULEY

> How women and men are now struggling with their
> changing consciousness about their "roles" as human
> beings in relation to each other marks a dramatic
> course similar to the changing consciousness of Jews
> and Christians about their "roles" as people of faith in
> relation to each other. . . . What the application of
> these parallels to interreligious dialogue means and
> will mean for Jewish-Christian relations may be as
> profound as what feminism has meant and still is com-
> ing to mean for American society as a whole.

Edward Flannery has written, "Every dialogist has his or
her own agenda or list of challenges. To a considerable
extent its composition will be determined by one's overall
evaluation of the merits or demerits of the twenty years
[since *Nostra Aetate*'s promulgation] we celebrate."[1]
Father Flannery is right on both counts, and the item at
the top of the list of challenges I bring to an evaluation of
the twenty years since *Nostra Aetate* is feminism. The
questions I consider are framed with reference to the
contributions a feminist perspective has to offer interreligious dialogue.

The critique of culture in the light of sexism and misogyny has startling and illuminating parallels to the cri-

tique of the historical relationship between Judaism and Christianity.[2] How women and men are now struggling with their changing consciousness about their "roles" as human beings in relation to each other marks a dramatic course similar to the changing consciousness of Jews and Christians about their "roles" as people of faith in relation to each other that has been developing in Christian and Jewish theological reflection since the Holocaust. Our recognition and understanding of these parallels are beginning to emerge only now in feminist discussions, conferences, small forums, and feminist publications. And, I am delighted to add, recognition of these parallels is being made explicit in the work of at least one key theoretician in the field of Jewish-Christian relations. I am referring to the work of Roy Eckardt and his forthcoming book, *Black-Woman-Jew: A Trinity of Liberation.*[3] What the application of these parallels to interreligious dialogue means and will mean for Jewish-Christian relations may be as profound as what feminism has meant and is still coming to mean for American society as a whole.

A formidable body of literature may be consulted for understanding the issues addressed by Jewish-Christian dialogue and by feminism. This literature has exploded in both fields since the early 1960s. The year 1963 saw the birth of the contemporary women's movement with the publication of Betty Freidan's *The Feminine Mystique*; 1965 saw the birth of contemporary Catholic-Jewish relations with the promulgation of the Second Vatican Council's *Nostra Aetate*. The following decade in the United States saw an unstoppable, irrevocable advance for both Jewish-Christian relations and feminism. Institutional structures began to respond and change. Windows and doors previously shut tight now began to open. In 1974, Rosemary Radford Ruether published *Faith and Fratricide*, her extraordinary challenge to the theology of Jewish-Christian relations, a challenge that was institutionally reinforced by the American Catholic bishops in 1975 with the "Guidelines" statement that

> There is here *a task incumbent on theologians, as yet hardly begun,* to explore the continuing relationship of the Jewish people with God and their spiritual bonds with the New Covenant and the fulfillment of God's plan for both Church and Synagogue.[4]

The key phrase in this context is "a task incumbent on theologians, as yet hardly begun."

Alan Davies writes in his Introduction to *Anti-Semitism and the Foundations of Christianity,* a 1979 collection of papers written in response to Ruether's work,

> Whatever its defects . . . , this work has succeeded in raising a host of biblical, theological and historical issues for Christian reflection through the daring and radical nature of its thesis: that anti-Judaism is the "left-hand" of classical Christology. In my judgment, it is Ruether's special contribution to have defined these issues in a manner that has redefined the problem itself.[5]

It is no accident that Ruether, who recognized and articulated issues that have prompted fruitful and absolutely necessary theological discourse on Jewish-Christian relations also pioneered feminist interpretations of Judaism and Christianity during the decade following the publication of *Faith and Fratricide.*[6] Her central role in both areas stems from the parallels between the critique of the historical relationship between Judaism and Christianity and the critique of culture in the light of sexism and misogyny.

In 1981, the Feminist Theological Institute[7] established a Task Force on Jewish-Christian Feminist Dialogue, thus giving a nurturing environment to a new genre of interreligious dialogue. I have served since 1981 as co-convenor of that Task Force along with Annette Daum, co-ordinator of Interreligious Affairs for the Union of American Hebrew Congregations (UAHC). Jewish-Christian feminist dialogue may be characterized as an emerging synthesis of Jewish-Christian dialogue and feminist interpretations of Christianity and Judaism. The Task Force's "statement of purpose" gives some insight into the self-understanding of this mode of dialogue:

> The Task Force begins from the premise that there is a unique historical relationship between Jews and Christians, and that Judaism and Christianity are two separate and distinct religious traditions. Feminists can and should have a significant role in promoting understanding and respect between Christians and Jews.
>
> The Task Force is disappointed that the feminist movement has sometimes unwittingly become a conduit for anti-Judaism. Many Christian women who are struggling to achieve equality and co-responsibility within their religious communities have adopted theological presuppositions that make biblical Judaism the source of misogyny and the oppression of women within Christianity and western civilization—and so once again make contemporary Jews and Judaism the "Other."
>
> The Task Force believes that Jewish and Christian feminists must first reach out to each other, in order to work together to help both of our religious traditions live up to the best that is within them. To this end the Task Force understands its purpose.

While it is apparent that the conciliatory institutional environment created for interreligious dialogue by *Nostra Aetate* has cleared the ground for Jewish-Christian feminist dialogue, at the same time many of the issues and concerns addressed by Jewish and Christian feminists engaged in interreligious dialogue are *not* touched by *Nostra Aetate* and are harbingers of areas dialogists still need to pursue. These areas focus directly on both the process and the content of interreligious dialogue, on the dialogue's own *praxis,* especially as defined and confined by the institutional frameworks through which almost all dialogue between Catholics and Jews has been conducted since *Nostra Aetate.*

In order to understand the potential contribution of Jewish-Christian feminist dialogue to the field of inter-religious relationships, one needs to be apprised of its origins and the reasons for its development in the feminist community. Jewish and Christian feminists are committed to dialogue with each other about feminism and religion but are not necessarily committed to interreligious dialogue about Jewish-Christian relations. Indeed, until quite recently, no distinction was made between feminist interreligious dialogue about feminism and feminist interreligious dialogue about Jewish-Christian relations, because the need for the former obscured the need for the latter. The issues addressed by the institutionalized process of interreligious dialogue and the issues addressed by Jewish and Christian feminists have been tangential, but neither set of issues has been integrated with the other. The channels through which most Jewish-Christian dialogue now operates are very much part of an "old boys' network," excluding both women and feminist interpretations of Judaism and Christianity. One need only ask the blatantly rhetorical questions, How many women were involved in the basic statement *Nostra Aetate*? How many women directly influenced the composition of the 1975 "Guidelines" and the 1985 "Notes"? How many women serve on the Vatican Commission for Religious Relations with the Jews? By the same token, how many women represent Jewish agencies and religious institutions on the International Jewish Committee on Interreligious Consultations (IJCIC)?[5] We understand that the goal of Catholic-Jewish relations is to establish and enhance relations between Catholics and Jews. Women comprise at least one-half of those constituencies. Women are at least as concerned about their relationship to God as are men, and probably more so with person-to-person human relationships.[9] An indispensable resource to the dialogue—and a significant part of the constituency Jewish-Christian dialogue is supposed to address—is slighted or ignored altogether by the institutional constraints imposed on interreligious dialogue.

Jewish-Christian feminist dialogue seeks to address what are, to date, two different endeavors: on the one hand, to bring a feminist perspective to interreligious dialogue about the relationship between Judaism and Christianity; on the other hand, to encourage interreligious dialogue between Jewish and Christian feminists. While interaction between Jewish and Christian feminists has been going on for some years now, what brings together most Jewish and Christian feminists thus far is our common bond as feminists and our mutual interest in feminist critiques of Judaism and Christianity. Although the feminist values bringing us together may be the same, our religious world views and historical experiences as women within our religious traditions are *not* the same. Except for the bond of feminism and the need to share feminist insights about our respective religious heritages through the inevitable overlap in our historical and theological explorations, Jewish and Christian feminists have been passing each other like ships in the night; inured to the problem of the historical relationship between Judaism and Christianity, while failing to confront and resolve these problems with other feminists through interreligious dialogue as Jews and Christians. As a consequence, the problem of anti-Semitism in the women's movement and the undercurrent of anti-Judaism in feminist commentary and scholarship are becoming more acute and are dividing Jewish and Christian feminists from each other. Jewish and Christian feminists, as Jews and Christians, are equally affected by the history of our traditions' mutual estrangement. The bond of feminism and the fact that Jewish and Christian feminists are a minority in our religious traditions are no longer sufficient reasons for us to overlook the fact that our efforts to eliminate sexism and misogyny in our religious traditions often inadvertently perpetuate religious prejudice between Christians and Jews.

What feminism has to contribute to interreligious dialogue and the need for interreligious dialogue among feminists is the dual focus of Jewish-Christian feminist dialogue. The first question bringing together many Jewish and Christian feminists was (and still is), "How might we survive as feminists in patriarchal religions?" From the encounters initiated by this question has developed the recognition for the need of Jewish-Christian feminist dialogue on interfaith relations. Feminists now turn their energies, commitment, and talent to such a dialogue, but find themselves at the stage of the "incipient issue." We straddle three conflicting hurdles: contemporary feminist scholarship on religion and culture, the abysmal history of Jewish-Christian relations over the millenia, and the grist of Jewish-Christian dialogue as defined thus far by the men who have gone before us.

From the 1960s to the present, interreligious dialogue between Catholics and Jews has been based on scholarship and theology and has been limited, for the most part, to clergy. Today, dialogue is still primarily in the hands of clergy—*male* clergy: neither the Roman Catholic Church nor Orthodox and (until February of 1985) Conservative Judaism ordain women.[10] As a consequence, very few women today are involved in Jewish-Christian dialogue. In addition, the almost exclusive focus on scholarship in interreligious dialogue has precluded the participation of many women, although this exclusion is not consciously deliberate. Historically, scholarship has been reserved for men in both the Christian and Jewish traditions. Christianity has propagated a world view dominated by mind-body dualism, with men as the minds and women as the bodies. In Judaism, the study of *Torah* and *Halakhah* traditionally have been reserved for men, with women as the enablers. Because women have been excluded from the processes which have given normative shape to our religious traditions—and to the values and world views which our traditions express—women have not been able to challenge until now those elements in our traditions which foster anti-Judaism and misogyny. Like Catholic-Jewish dialogue since the promulgation of *Nostra Aetate,* the involvement of women in the dialogue process is, in the words of the prophet Jeremiah, "a new thing in the earth" (Jer. 31:22b).[11]

Some who are drawn to interfaith dialogue between Jewish and Christian feminists are feminists actively committed to Jewish-Christian relations. Many more are Christian and Jewish feminists who are coming to interfaith dialogue for the first time out of their deep commitment to their own religious traditions and out of their need to find encouragement and support from feminists in other religious traditions, who, like themselves, are actively working to achieve equality for women and co-responsibility within their faith communities and religious institutions.[12] Most are not clergy or scholars. Most do not possess "Rabbi" or "Reverend" before their names, with "Ph.D." bringing up the rear for good measure. As a consequence, most feminists concerned with interfaith dialogue with other feminists and with those already engaged in interreligious dialogue do not possess the credentials necessary to gain access to and to influence the dialogue process that has been established almost exclusively through the channels of academic and religious institutions.

Out of their experiences as feminists within their religious traditions, some Jewish and Christian feminists of faith[13] are now working together to create a genre of interreligious dialogue that will help to refocus the issues dominating the history of Jewish-Christian relations. We are working to refocus these issues by bringing the heretofore "alien" factor of *women's* experiences, aspirations, and women's historical consciousness to interfaith dialogue and to examine, through feminist hermeneutics, religious practices, and theological concepts such as "covenant" that are of particular concern in interfaith dialogue.

The Task Force on Jewish-Christian Feminist Dialogue has a motto: "We must understand what was, in order to change what is, and so effect what is to be." Many feminists accuse religion of being the seed-bed for the sexism and misogyny experienced in western cultures and they trace its origins to a Judaic heritage. Even feminists who are not "religious," both Jews and nonJews, have picked up this anti-Judaic thrust and internalized it. Those efforts at feminist scholarship which have contributed so much to the self-understanding of Jewish and Christian feminists have been, to date, the work mostly of Christians. Tragically, through these same efforts has emerged the ancient voice of anti-Judaism which operates within Christianity at best at a subliminial level, and which has been prevalent in the women's movement since the time of the suffragists, as so blatantly presented in Elizabeth Cady Stanton's *The Woman's Bible* (1895). Jewish feminists have had the painful task of making Christian feminists aware of the often unwitting anti-Judaism reflected in their scholarship and commentary.[14] Our recognition of anti-Judaic attitudes in Christian and post-Christian feminist writings has been a major force behind the incipient issue of Jewish-Christian feminist dialogue.

FEMINISM AND THE DYNAMIC OF
INTERRELIGIOUS DIALOGUE

How anti-Judaism damages the contributions of feminist hermeneutics on religion is, however, only one
aspect of Jewish-Christian feminist dialogue. At the same
time, through these chastening efforts at self-
examination, an awareness is emerging that feminist
theory and practice have much to contribute to understanding the dynamic of interreligious dialogue and the
history of Jewish-Christian relations. Through
Jewish-Christian feminist dialogue, we are beginning to
see the corners into which our respective traditions have
painted themselves and the factors which undercut the
efforts of dialogue in interfaith relations. These same
"corners"—the "theology" of religious triumphalism, for
example—are those which feminists of faith see as major
barriers to the equality and co-responsibility of women as
actors and participants in their religious traditions.

Jewish and Christian feminists of faith see the challenge of claiming the fullness of their humanity and the
co-equal responsibilities this claim entails as unique to
and made possible by the times in which they are living.
This challenge requires that they call their religious
traditions to accountability beyond mere resolutions
made "in principle" for enacting the affirmation of a
vision of humanness grounded in the normative values
of both traditions.

Given the extent to which the normative values of
Judaism and Christianity clash with cultural visions of
humanness that make one sex (or race, or class) more
human *and* divine than the "Other," the identification of
these oppressive cultural visions with Jewish and Christian normative values undermines the credibility of these
traditions' contributions to the world as much as any
other abuse. The problem is one of conflicting visions or
models of humanness operating within both Judaism

and Christianity and their institutionalized expressions. The critique of this problem by feminist hermeneutics "from within" is helping to bring about a re-formation, a re-creation, a new birth in the self-understandings of our religious traditions. In turn, a rebirth in self-understanding is bringing about a redefinition of our traditions' relationship to each other and to the world, a relational transformation to which Jewish-Christian feminist dialogue has much to contribute. In conversation with each other, Christian and Jewish feminists are beginning to apply the insights of feminist theory's "patriarchal morality of projection" to Jewish-Christian relations.[15] This morality has been historically acted out as religious triumphalism, a destructive phenomenon operative in both traditions and which clearly shows up in the institutional dialogue process between Christians and Jews over key theological issues such as "covenant" and "election."

THE 1985 "NOTES" ON PREACHING AND CATECHESIS: A THREEFOLD PROBLEM

I will discuss these issues within the context of the 1985 "Notes on the Correct Way to Present Jews and Judaism in Preaching and Catechesis in the Roman Catholic Church." While there is certainly much to commend the "Notes" as a contemporary document of an ancient, institutionally self-defined religious construct, at the same time the "Notes" illustrate the areas addressed by the Jewish-Christian feminist dialogue with regard to the content and the process of interreligious dialogue. Extensive critiques of the "Notes" by both Catholics and Jews have been circulated since the document's release on June 24, 1985, some published, some not. My purpose is not to offer yet another point-by-point analysis, but to make some overall comments about the "Notes" from a feminist perspective as the document reflects on the current state of the dialogue between Catholics and Jews in the post-history of *Nostra Aetate*.

It is true that the "Notes" are written by and for the Church, that they are a product of consensus within the teaching magisterium about Jews and Judaism and are not intended as a consultative product of interreligious dialogue. At the same time what the "Notes" purport to do and what they in fact accomplish are distinct from one another. Here we are dealing with the "Notes" as a product of the *process* of interreligious dialogue, for the "Notes" take as precursors the 1975 "Guidelines" and *Nostra Aetate*. Indeed we are to understand the "Notes" in part as the Church's twentieth anniversary gift to *Nostra Aetate* and the era of Catholic-Jewish dialogue it has initiated.

At the beginning of the document, in paragraph 4 of section I (entitled "Religious Teaching and Judaism"), the "Notes" bid us to

> recall the passage in which the "Guidelines and Suggestions" tried to define the fundamental condition of dialogue: "respect for the other as he is," knowledge of the "basic components of the religious tradition of Judaism" and again learning "by what essential traits the Jews define themselves in the light of their own religious experience."

What the "Notes" purport to do with regard to "the fundamental condition of dialogue" and what is accomplished are tragically representative of the weakest areas of the dialogue process within its current institutional frameworks. As a document, the "Notes" do not try to understand the Jew "as he is," nor do the "Notes" present Jews' self-definition "in the light of their own religious experience." Instead, the "Notes" are a document which shows how to fit Jews and Judaism into Catholic teaching. Indeed, the document is a portrait of Judaism's "role" in the Church, and that role is subordinated within the larger designs of the Church's own salvific self-understanding. The extent to which Jews are defined in the "Notes" by non-dialogic theological constructs borders on Christian triumphalism. Similarly, the Church's recent statements on women over the past decade[16] have little to do with how women see themselves and their relationship with God, and everything to do with how the Church fits women and women's religious self-understanding into traditional Catholic teaching about women and women's "role" in the Church.

The difference in the process between how the Church addresses Jews and Judaism and how the Church addresses women in the post-*Nostra Aetate* era has created in Catholic-Jewish relations the hopeful expectation of dialogic trust and respect for the "Other." The outcry and dismay of the international leadership representing Jewish agencies and religious institutions about not being consulted during the three-year process through which the "Notes" were created is more than understandable. The difference is, women do not even think of making a concerted protest when it comes to the formulation of theological positions that have impact on women, because we are not involved in the process to begin with. What is at stake here is the power of naming. You cannot talk *about* someone unless you also are willing to talk *with* them. The battle for women to reclaim the power of naming within religious tradition is hardly yet begun.

Let us now turn our attention to the content of the "Notes" as generally representative of the current state of the content of interreligious dialogue as framed by religious institutions. Many will agree that the "Notes" are indicative of three major problems: triumphalism, typology, and a more conservative approach to theology in general.

TRIUMPHALISM

The problem of triumphalism[17] clearly shows up in the dialogue process when it comes to Jews and Christians discussing the nature of their convenant relationship with God. Although the critique of the "Notes" with regard to triumphalism is potentially extensive, I shall limit my discussion of triumphalism and the "Notes" to the issue of covenant. For Jews and Christians, affirming each other's convenantal validity, mutuality, and autonomy has been the most difficult and the most important theological issue in contemporary Jewish-Christian dialogue since the mid-1970s. While affirming "in principle" the inclusiveness of Christianity's and Judaism's separate and distinct traditions about their covenant relationship with God (meaning that the one's covenant does not necessarily exclude the other's), the exclusiveness of Jews' and Christians' historical self-understanding of their covenant with God dominates and undermines many recent efforts to engage in interreligious dialogue on covenant.[18]

Some of the recent and most creative theological work in Jewish-Christian relations has focused on the problem of covenant.[19] A number of alternative formulations have been proposed, such as two parallel but mutually affirming covenant traditions, or a single covenant with two branches. The "Notes" ignore the current scholarship and back themselves into a corner in their simplistic attempt to affirm the "spiritual bonds" linking Judaism and Christianity. Since we have such bonds, and since "Jesus affirms that 'there shall be one flock and one shepherd,'" the "Church and Judaism cannot then be seen as two parallel ways of salvation and the church must witness to Christ as the redeemer for all . . . " ("Notes" I:7). The Vatican "Notes" tell us that there cannot be two parallel covenants, and yet, as Eugene Fisher writes in his analysis, the document "does not offer its own model for the relationship. As with previous documents, there is much that remains unresolved for the dialogue."[20]

This opens up several questions within the document about covenant, the most basic being, "What do the "Notes" mean?" If the covenants of Judaism and Christianity cannot be separate and parallel, then they have to meet somewhere and diverge somewhere. The "Notes" say that there cannot be two separate covenants because Judaism and Christianity are related. If this is true, then what *is* the relationship? If they are related, is one the offshoot of the other? In its attempt to affirm a relationship it is unable (or unwilling) to describe, the Vatican "Notes" through their typological language manage to create the impression of a linear, hierarchical vision of covenant, reserving the status of the Church above that of the Synagogue. This stumble is a result of the tendency in Jewish-Christian dialogue, when there is discourse on covenant, to emphasize the issues of "election" and "exclusivity," a tendency which has poisoned the well of dialogue for both Jews and Christians.

Christian and Jewish feminists have become aware of the psychological focus on election and exclusivity in discussions of covenant in their attempt to ask of the dialogue what is for them the basic question: "Just what does a concept such as covenant and the religious reality it fosters mean in terms of human experience?" Feminists look at how the metaphors of our religious traditions for covenant foment against the equality and co-responsibility of women in the covenant relationship our traditions claim is normative for human beings. Since only men are allowed to fulfill the religious duties our traditions have elaborated, men must be more "elect" than women (meaning only men are permitted full participation). Our religious traditions have understood the "Other's" place in the covenant relationship in similar terms. While each tradition believes that it bears greater responsibility than any "Other" in in the scheme of God's covenantal purposes, our covenant traditions do not totally exclude the "Other." The "Other" is elect somehow, but "we," who are either born or baptized into greater responsibility, are closer to God. Hierarchical constructs serve as the interpretive matrix for covenant in both Judaism and Christianity. For both Catholic-Jewish dialogue and for women in each religious tradition, such an interpretive matrix is inadequate. Feminists of faith propose that *hesed* [mercy], not hierarchy, needs to be our primary interpretive matrix for covenant.

TYPOLOGY

If anti-Semitism is the left-hand of Christology, then certainly typology is the left-hand of triumphalism. Typology is rooted in a signifier-signified approach to language. That which signifies something has meaning and significance only in relation to what is signified. If, as the "Notes" seem to portray, Jews exist in Catholic teaching and preaching only as a precursor to Christianity, then Jews have no significance beyond that. This parallels the way women exist in relation to men. In both Catholicism and Judaism, women service men. Women have no meaningful and significant existence apart from what they signify in relation to men. The imagery of marriage is often used in Scripture and tradition to express the covenant relationship between God and Israel and God and the Church, but the historical assumption behind the imagery is women's subjection to men and men's enlarged responsibilities in patriarchal societies. For both the dialogue and for feminists of faith, the language of typology is not only inadequate, it is unacceptable, regardless of its liturgical significance for the Church, especially during the seasons of Advent and Lent.

CONSERVATIVE THEOLOGY

A more conservative approach to theology in general is a third problem area with regard to the "Notes" and what the document bodes for dialogue at the level of religious institutions. This is probably the most serious of all problems, for contemporary dialogue has been grounded in the work of contemporary theology. The parallels are immediate between feminist interpretations of Judaism and Christianity and the critique of the historical relationship between the two. The more conservative the theology, the less equality for women in *any* theological system across the board. The more conservative the theology, the "older" it is, the more traditional, which has always placed more importance on the role of men—be it in Islam, Judaism, or Christianity. This parallels what happens in Jewish-Christian relations. The more conservative the theology, generally speaking, the less egalitarian it will be, not only towards women but towards other religious systems. With regard to Christian tradition, the more conservative, the more triumphalist. After all, the theological exploration of a double-covenant theory, or more than one approach to covenant relationship, or more than one people of God, is fairly recent and comes out of liberal theological traditions.

Fortunately for both the dialogue and for feminists of faith, the "Notes" are not the last word on Catholic-Jewish relations. A report issued July 23, 1985, by a Catholic-Jewish consulation on the Vatican "Notes," and signed by representatives of the dialogue in some Jewish agencies and Catholic institutions, concludes with the statement, "We will work to ensure that the "Notes" will not be the occasion of a retreat from the very real gains in mutual understanding achieved in the past twenty years."[21] Such a statement of affirmation *is* the heritage of *Nostra Aetate*. What needs to be accomplished is the job that the "Notes" say they are going to do, and that is to put into Catholic teaching information about how Jews define themselves. It is because of what has and has not happened in Jewish-Christian dialogue that Christian and Jewish feminists are particularly sensitive to the issue of self-definition and how crucial it is in any communication process. Women in both communities need to be involved in the process of self-definition in the dialogue between Christians and Jews. These concerns are taken up in a movement, still in its incipient stages of development, named "Jewish-Christian feminist dialogue."

NOTES

1. Edward H. Flannery, "The Challenges We Jointly Face: A Catholic View," *Face to Face: An Interreligious Bulletin* (Anti-Defamation League of B'nai B'rith), vol. 12 (Fall 1985): p. 45.

2. Portions of this essay are excerpted from an article by Deborah McCauley and Annette Daum, "Jewish-Christian Feminist Dialogue: A Wholistic Vision," *Union Seminary Quarterly Review* 38/2 (1983): pp. 147–190.

3. A. Roy Eckardt, *Black-Woman-Jew: A Trinity of Liberation,* to be published by Indiana University Press.

4. Declaration of the U.S. National Conference of Catholic Bishops, Nov. 20, 1975 (italics added).

5. Alan T. Davies, ed., *Anti-Semitism and the Foundations of Christianity* (New York: Paulist Press, 1979), p. xvi.

6. Rosemary Radford Ruether, ed., *Religion and Sexism: Images of Woman in the Jewish and Christian Traditions* (New York: Simon and Schuster, 1974). *Religion and Sexism* is still the standard survey and was published the same year as *Faith and Fratricide.*

7. The Feminist Theological Institute (FTI) was founded in 1980 and is a national network of support and "a resource for those who are *unapologetically both feminist and religious*" (statement of purpose). The FTI consists of local and interest groups.

8. Annette Daum, co-ordinator of Interreligious Affairs for the Union of American Hebrew Congregations (UAHC), is

currently the only woman serving on IJCIC who heads a department of interreligious affairs for a Jewish agency.

9. The significance of sex differences in approaches to moral dilemmas (and applicable to theological issues) such as those posed by Jewish-Christian dialogue is explored in the work of Carol Gilligan, *In a Different Voice: Psychological Theory and Women's Development* (Cambridge, Mass.: Harvard University Press, 1982). See Annette Daum, "A Jewish Feminist View," *Theology Today* 41/3 (October 1984): pp. 298–299.

10. On October 24, 1983, the faculty voted to admit women to the rabbinical college of the Jewish Theological Seminary of America, thus making women eligible for training and ordination by the Seminary. The Rabbinical Assembly (the organization of Conservative rabbis in the U.S. and Canada) announced in February 1985 that it would admit to membership anyone ordained by the seminary, male or female, thus completing the official movement towards women's ordination begun in 1983. The Reform movement has ordained women to the rabbinate since 1972. Already, about half of the rabbinical candidates at Reform and Reconstructionist seminaries are women.

11. For a feminist interpretation of Jeremiah 31:15–22 and the significance of v. 22b, see Phyllis Trible, *God and the Rhetoric of Sexuality* (Philadelphia: Fortress Press, 1978), pp. 40–50.

12. These efforts to achieve mutual co-responsibility for women in religion involve a critique of their traditions' sexism in attitudes, actions, and institutional structures by which women as persons and as a group are subordinated on grounds of sex and gender in religious language, symbolism, theology, ethics, and practice. Although Jewish and Christian feminists face the same fundamental problems within our respective traditions, we have to deal with very different particulars and perspectives embodying these problems in our individual faith communities.

13. The description "feminists of faith" is an attempt to avoid the divisive dichotomy of "secular feminists" versus "religious feminists." It means to describe those feminists for whom the language of religion—and for many this denotes the language of their religious traditions—is integral to their self-understanding and world view.

14. Judith Plaskow, "Blaming Jews for Inventing Patriarchy," *Lilith*, no. 7 (1981): pp. 11–12; Annette Daum, "Blaming Jews for the Death of the Goddess," *Lilith*, no. 7 (1981): pp. 12–13; "Feminists and Faith: A Discussion with Judith Plaskow and Annette Daum," *Lilith*, No. 7 (1981), pp. 14–17; Annette Daum, "Anti-Semitism in the Women's Movement," *Pioneer Woman* (The Women's Labor Zionist Organization of America) 28/4 (September-October 1983): pp. 11ff; McCauley and Daum, "Jewish-Christian Feminist Dialogue," pp. 173–182. See also Letty Cottin Pogrebin, "Anti-Semitism in the Women's Movement," *Ms.* (June 1982): pp. 45ff.

15. The theoretical formulation of the "patriarchal morality of projection" has its origins in the work of Mary Daly. Patriarchal projection is the attributing of one's own failures, weaknesses, and insufficiencies to another who is usually perceived to be less powerful. The one who is the object of these projections thus becomes the primary "Other" who is then blamed for the consequences of these insufficiencies. In terms of human social systems, feminists understand that women have been and continue to be seen as the primary "Other" of patriarchal projection. Patriarchal projection is embodied in the historical relationship between Judaism and Christianity. Judaism has always been the primary "Other" onto which Christianity has projected those parts of itself to which it will not lay claim. In this scenario, Judaism becomes the bad parent whom Christianity as the adult child blames and punishes for those parts of its personality it does not like and for which it refuses to accept responsibility. The patriarchal morality of projection is applicable to the phenomenon of feminist anti-Judaism; see McCauley and Daum, "Jewish-Christian Feminist Dialogue," pp. 182–184.

16. The single most significant document is the Vatican's statement on the ordination of women, *Declaration on the Question of the Ordination of Women to the Ministerial Priesthood* (Washington, D.C.: U.S. Catholic Conference, 1976).

17. Religious triumphalism may be perpetuated only through the marginalization of "Others." Triumphalism in any form fosters an attitude of oneupmanship, and may be described in terms of knowledge and power over others. The

triumphalistic exercise of knowledge and power is characterized by a self-conscious accountability to those of equal or
greater authority, but not to those who are subject to the
unilateral exercise of such authority. Triumphalism enshrines
a pattern or system of authority within hierarchical structures
which makes one class of people more important (often meaning "better than"), more powerful, and therefore more entitled to dominate than another (the authority of clergy over
laity, male over female). This same system carries over to
relations between institutions, which vie with one another for
power and dominance in relation to each other (*my* religious
tradition over *your* religious tradition, *my* covenant with God
over *your* covenant with God). In terms of religious institutions,
religious triumphalism may be identified in large part with
clericalism, the domination of ordained clergy over the religious self-understanding and participation of others in their
own faith traditions. For an "insider's" analysis of the problems
of clericalism and suggestions for change, see Thomas H.
Groome, "From Chauvinism and Clericalism to Priesthood:
The Long March," in *Women and Religion: A Reader for the
Clergy,* ed. Regina Coll (New York: Paulist Press, 1982).

18. An example of the intrusion of the concepts "election"
and exclusivity on interreligious discussions of covenant clearly shows up in a still widely used pamphlet, *Covenant or Covenants? A Historical Reflection on the Notion of Covenant* (1979),
published by the Los Angeles Priest-Rabbi Committee. For a
feminist analysis of the pamphlet, see McCauley and Daum,
"Jewish-Christian Feminist Dialogue," pp. 161–163. See also
Annette Daum, "A Jewish Feminist View."

19. See especially John Pawlikowski, *What Are They Saying
about Christian-Jewish Relations* (New York: Paulist Press, 1980),
the chapter "Theology and Covenant." See also Pawlikowski,
Christ in the Light of the Christian-Jewish Dialogue (New York:
Paulist Press, 1982); and Paul van Buren, *Discerning the Way: A
Theology of the Jewish-Christian Reality,* 2 vol. (New York: Seabury Press, 1980, 1983). For Jewish interpretations of covenant, see Helga Croner and Leon Klenicki, eds., *Issues in the
Jewish-Christian Dialogue: Jewish Perspectives on Covenant, Mission
and Witness* (New York: Paulist Press, 1979); David Novak,

"The Covenants We Share: A Jewish Perspective," *Face to Face*: *An Interreligious Bulletin* (Anti-Defamation League of B'nai B'rith), vol. 12 (Fall 1985): pp. 37ff.

20. Eugene J. Fisher, "Vatican Commission 'Notes' on Catechesis and Preaching," July 1985: p. 15. Paper circulated out of the Office of the Secretariat for Catholic-Jewish Relations, National Conference of Catholic Bishops.

21. Press release, U.S. Catholic Conference News, "Catholic, Jewish Leaders Ask Continued Dialogue in Light of Vatican Statement," July 23, 1985. Press release, American Jewish Committee, July 23, 1985.

Contributors

ROGER BROOKS is Assistant Professor of Theology at the University of Notre Dame and teaches Judaica in the Christianity and Judaism in Antiquity program. His research, which focuses on early Rabbinic literature in its cultural context, currently includes a study of Jewish and Christian understandings of the Bible in the first four centuries.

DAVID B. BURRELL, C.S.C., is Professor of Philosophy and Professor of Theology at the University of Notre Dame. He served for one year as Rector of the Ecumenical Institute for Theological Research in Jerusalem, where he pursued studies in Jewish and Islamic philosophical theology. He is author of *Knowing the Unknowable God: Ibn-Sina, Maimonides, and Aquinas,* recently published by the University of Notre Dame Press.

WENDELL S. DIETRICH is Professor of Religious Studies and Professor of Judaic Studies at Brown University in Providence, Rhode Island. His current research interest is in late nineteenth- and early twentieth-century Protestant and Roman Catholic thought and the relation of this to German Judaic thought in the same period.

EDWARD H. FLANNERY is Director of the Office of Continuing Education of the Clergy for the diocese of Providence, Rhode Island, as well as President of the National Christian Leadership Conference for Israel. He is author of *Anguish of the Jews: Twenty-Three Centuries of Anti-Semitism,* an award winning and seminal study of the roots of this perennial theological problem.

DEBORAH VANSAU MCCAULEY serves as Co-Convenor of the Task Force on Jewish Christian Feminist Dialogue and has written articles on women and religion, including "The Bible and Women: People, Language, Imagery, and God" (with Kathryn Piccard) and "Jewish-Christian Feminist Dialogue: A Wholistic Vision" (with Annette Daum).

JOHN T. PAWLIKOWSKI, O.S.M., serves as Professor of Social Ethics at the Chicago Theological Union, is a member of the U.S. Holocaust Memorial Council, and author of a recent volume on Christology in the light of Jewish-Christian relations, *Christ in the Light of the Christian-Jewish Dialogue.*

ABRAHAM J. PECK is Administrative Director of the American Jewish Archives of the Hebrew Union College-Jewish Institute of Religion in Cincinnati. He is editor of *Jews and Christians after the Holocaust,* a member of the International Advisory Board of the International Center for Holocaust Studies of the Anti-Defamation League of B'nai B'rith, and a founding member of the Cincinnati Interfaith Holocaust Foundation.

DANIEL F. POLISH is the Senior Rabbi of Temple Israel in Hollywood, California, and teaches in the Department of Religious Studies at Occidental College. He has served as Associate Executive Vice President and Director of the

Washington, D.C. office of the Synagogue Council of America, and is co-editor of *The Formation of Social Policy in the Catholic and Jewish Traditions* and *The Liturgical Foundations of Social Policy in the Catholic and Jewish Traditions* (both from University of Notre Dame Press).

MICHAEL A. SIGNER is Professor of Jewish History at the Hebrew Union College-Jewish Institute of Religion in Los Angeles. An expert in Medieval Jewish literature, he was consultant to the Exhibition of Vatican Library Hebraica in the United States of America. He also has written widely on Jewish-Christian relations in medieval and modern times, including "Thirteenth-Century Christian Hebraism: The Commentary on Canticles ascribed to Andrew of St. Victor" and the forthcoming edition of *Andreas de Sancto Victore, Expositio in Iezechielem Prophetam.*

THOMAS F. STRANSKY, C.S.P., was a founding staff member of the Vatican's Secretariat for Promoting Christian Unity (1960–1970), and a participant in all phases of the drafting of *Nostra Aetate.* Past President of the Paulist Fathers, he is now director of Paulist candidates at the Novitiate in Oak Ridge, New Jersey.

Index of Biblical Verses

215

Index of Names

Index of Subjects